ECONOMIC DISTORTION DYNAMICS

Copyright © 2017 by Raoul Kennedy

All rights reserved.

This book or any portion thereof may not be reproduced or used in any manner whatsoever without the express written permission of the publisher except for the use of brief quotations in a book review.

ISBN-13: 978-1976404092

ISBN-10: 1976404096

Dedicated to my family for their patience

TABLE OF CONTENTS

INTRODUCTION... 1
    Summary of Book Structure
    Qualifications and Shortcomings

PART I. A CONCEPTUAL MODEL... 2

Overview... 3
System 1 Fundamental Cost-Return Coupling Bond
System 2 Decoupling Process and Distortions
Subsystems and Tables
Most Dangerous Potential Outcomes: Detail
Polarity
Linkage: Fundamental Cost-Return Decoupling

Economy: System 1 Architecture... 8
Table of Characteristics and Detail
Building Block: Fundamental Cost-Return Coupling Bond
    Cost and Return Detail
        Parallel with Energy
    Voluntary Dispossession
    Proportionality
    Disproportionality
    Other References to a Coupling Bond Concept

System Features... 12
    Economization
    Voluntary production/selling

Accounting for Economization and Selling... 13
    Net Benefit (Returns) Accounting
        Revenues
        Return and Cost within the Coupling Bond
        Justice and Origins of Cost Avoidance

Perspectives on Economization... 15
    Deflation
    Human Ingenuity and Economization of Time
    Rates of Return

> The Threat of AI and Economization
> Variations in Propensity to Economize
> Qualifications and Clarifications
>> Money Optional vs. Practical
> Sustainability and Future Trends

Wealth Accumulation via Compounding... 20
> Future Orientation (Future Value)
>> Variables
>>> Economization in r: Net Cash Flow
>>> Economization in r: Cost Reductions
>>>> Scenarios: 1; 2 a, b
>>> Compounding and the term e
>> Other Compounding Periods
>>> Wealth-Building: Financial Instruments
> Other Clarifications
>> Cash Flow Emphasis
>> Ethics and Wealth Accumulation

Use of Force
Policies in System 1
Polarity and Feedback Loop
> Diagram

Linkages: System 1 to System 2 Decoupling Process... 29
Income-Based Fees and Components
> Principal/Agent Problem and Incentives
>> 1. Commensurate/Voluntary;
>> 2. Decoupling: Involuntary
Comparative Polarity and Feedback Loops
> Diagram
Derivative Inflows to System 2: Overview

Derivative Inflows: System 2 Architecture... 35
Table of Characteristics
Decoupling Dynamics
Entities Detail

Income Sources

Overview of Subsystems of System 2... 37
Table: System 2 Inflows and Subsystems
Polarity and Feedback Loop
Diagram
Table: Feedback Loop Summary
Financing of Subsystem Activities: Detail
Administration and Interventions: Detail
    Bureaucracy
    Administrative Law

Phases of Dominant Feedback Loops... 44
Initial Phase: Reinforcing
Subsequent Phases: Overshoot-Reversal
Forecasted Timeframe of Loops
Acceleration of Feedback Loops
Use of Force in System 2
Wealth Accumulation in System 2

Emergence of Economic Distortions... 48
Origins
    Cost-Return Decoupling
    Cost-Return Disproportionality
    Perception Management
Embodiment of Distortions
    Prices as Signals
    Distortion-Embodied Prices and Costs
Cost-Return Decoupling and Disproportionality: Other Points
    Deadweight Costs
    Immutability (Lack of Opt-Out)
Comparison of Systemic Distortions
    System 2-Originated
    System 1-Originated
        Examples: Natural disasters, Asset markets

Part II. SUBSYSTEM AND POLICY TABLES... 56

Column Categories: Feedback Loop Progression... 56
Columns A through N... 56
A. Policy Intervention Type
B. Level/Scale
C. Rhetorical Justification
D. Decoupling: Returns portion. Wealth gains (via the offering of political and financial support); income/Wealth distorted upwards.
E. Decoupling: Costs portion. Cost-Bearers: bearing the cost (et incomes/wealth reduced).
Phase 1 (Initial)... 56
F. Rent-Seeking Activity
G. Impaired Production/Reduced Income Impacts
H. Shortages (including food crises)
I. Black Markets and violence due to contract non-legality
J. Clustering: Oversupply/Excessive Speculation and Competition
Delay 1-Overshoot... 56
K. Deficit/Debt (Expenditures>Inflows)
Delay 2-Reversal (also possible S-Curve or Collapse)... 56
L. Secondary Policies/Impacts (including state violence)
M. Ownership Insecurity (including self-ownership); hoarding
N. Visible Protests/Unrest

Subsystem 1: Derivative Inflows and Redistribution... 79
Policy Table... 80
Policy Interventions... 83
Sub1.1
Sub1.2
Sub1.3
Sub1.4
Sub1.5
Sub1.6

Subsystem 2: Fiat Law—Other Overriding Interventions... 94
Policy Table... 94
Policy Interventions... 97

Sub2.1
Sub2.2
Sub2.3
Sub2.4
Sub2.5
Sub2.6

Subsystem 3: Overriding Interventions—Fiat Money... 126
Policy Table... 127
Policy Interventions... 130
Sub3.1
Sub3.2
Sub3.3
Sub3.4
Sub3.5
Sub3.6

APPENDICES: PERSPECTIVES... 151

A1. Prices, Costs, and Loss... 151
Price Controls
Fairness Policy Interventions
Price Controls and Realities
    Loss
    Market Logic: Economic and Political
    Morality of Markets: Economic and Political
        Crisis and Continued Supply
        Asymmetry in Cost-Return
        Antifragility and Political Markets
        Policy and Cost-Return Disproportionality

Distorted Prices and Costs: Examples...
    Shortages and Losses
    Oversupply and Losses
Price and Cost: Non-Money Illustration
    Producing Alone
    Trade/Exchange
    Time-Saving Technology

A2. Ideology, Morality, and Political Systems... 164
Policy Formulation and the Social Justice Imperative
Morality and Fairness Ideologies
    Analysis of Injustice
        Rhetoric and Labels vs. Actual Policies
Historical Record of Fairness Ideologies: Theory and Practice
    Fairness Policy in Other Modern Systems
Ideologies Advocating Reduced State Intervention
    Individualism vs. Collectivism
Future Policy Risks
    Pensions and the Overshoot
    Belief Systems
    Intransigent Minorities

A3. Wealth Accumulation: Alternative Scenarios... 174
Zero Rate of Return
Negative (Real) Rate of Return
Total Wealth Destruction
Nothing to Invest (Illustration)
    Innovation and the Physics of Economics
Investing: Three Cases
    1. Tax and Inflation Ignored
    2. Moderate Inflation and Taxes
    3. Higher Inflation, Taxes Unchanged
        Deflation
A Business Entity

INTRODUCTION

What if we had a rough reference to make sense of the world and why some bad things happen. Drawing from economic theory and system dynamics, a conceptual model is explored in which economic distortions stem from returns that are disproportionate to cost-bearing. Policies responsible for such distortions can generate feedback loops that raise the risk of dislocation and tragic outcomes, including shortages and food crises, environmental damage, oversupply and waste, unjust wealth and impoverishment, asset bubble-crash cycles, violence, and human rights abuses. Moreover, the dynamics suggest an unsustainable path which threatens hardship for those of us who are dependent upon the current paradigm.

Insights into complex economic systems are a vital first step towards sustainability and social justice. The potential dangers of certain interventions reviewed here invoke the *precautionary principle*-- avoiding policy action when the impacts are systemic. It is hoped that the ideas presented can serve as a resource for anyone seeking a bigger picture in planning for the future.

Summary of Book Structure. The book is divided into three major parts which include the Appendices. Part I concerns the overall conceptual model which after a brief overview is divided into the system architecture and the linkages between the two basic systems: System 1 (Economy) and System 2 (Derivative Inflows). Part II, Subsystem and Policy Tables, focuses on the three subsystems of System 2 and the specific policies of each subsystem. The appendices offer additional explanations, illustrations, and perspectives on some of the topics discussed in the main text.

Qualifications and Shortcomings. This document began as a notebook to help explain economic and financial events and their proximate causes based upon economic theory. The analysis evolved into a conceptual model drawing upon system dynamics and other disciplines. Unexpectedly, it became clearer that the analysis could be applied to violence and human rights abuses.

It is recognized that the theorized link between policy and outcomes may be weak or inconsistent – undoubtedly exceptions exist in which policies were implemented that did not result in outcomes as suggested by the model. At best, because of complexity and non-linearities, some *tendency* for certain outcomes is thought to exist. In addition, because proper treatment of the subject matter requires a broad range of expertise, this research might be viewed as an incomplete rough draft. Redundancies may be common due to the interrelationships and similarities between certain policies and their outcomes, as well as disorganization. Despite these failings, as well as typos and errors, omissions and oversights, misinterpretations, contradictions, oversimplifications, and lastly, writing style, hopefully elements of this work might contribute towards solving some of our greatest problems. Technical parts familiar to readers can be skipped over, although it is hoped that the creative, perhaps odd, illustrations might be interesting and useful. The reader is encouraged to consult other resources on individual topics to supplement an understanding of the material presented here; terms in *italics* and the abbreviation "Re:" are added to assist with this. Conventions adopted in the book and other notes are found in an Addendum before the References.

PART I. A CONCEPTUAL MODEL

When we watch or read the news or report covering an important issue, without economic theory and a systems approach we may not be aware whether the event or issue is part of a logical sequence or a causal chain within an entire system. Is the event a *symptom* of (a) (previous) *cause*(s)? Is the event a catalyst for something else that might occur? Moving along some hypothetical path, what might be the final phase(s) and outcome(s)? A conceptual model might help us answer some of these questions.

A model is crude representation of what might explain the world around us: An inherently unpredictable non-linear infinitely complex reality that is necessarily incorrect due to the limits of our knowledge. Drawing from historical observations, economic theory and concepts from various disciplines including system dynamics and complexity theory, the aim of this model is to generate a working idea of the likelihood of the outcomes of policy interventions into economic systems (Hayek 1945; Sayama 2015). Policy interventions may in some cases be well-intentioned but the *precautionary principle* bears mentioning here: To avoid taking actions that may have system-wide effects when the dynamics are not clearly understood (Taleb 2010). It is truly hoped that this model can shed some light on the importance of avoidance to prevent the most dangerous outcomes that policy interventions may cause.

Moreover, the sustainability of systems is also crucial because however moral and just the system may be intended to be, if the system is inherently unsustainable, leading to either reversal or collapse, *those dependent upon the system will suffer*, and resulting dislocations could pose new threats to all.

Overview

The diagrams below begin with a theorized fundamental (*cost-return*) *coupling bond* of System 1 – the coupling of cost borne and associated returns—followed by the process and nature of System 2 interventions into the economic system, resulting in economic distortions and possible outcomes.

System 1 Fundamental Cost-Return Coupling Bond. This bond is thought of as a type of building block of the system such that *returns* are bound to *cost-bearing* --the *costs borne* to generate that return; this also defines a principle of ownership of the return. The reverse is also true that full ownership of the return implies full ownership of the *costs* associated with that return; in other words, full responsibility, and accountability.

System 2 Decoupling Process and Distortions

Various interventions originating from System 2 are defined as *decoupling* interventions, beginning with a *fundamental* cost-return decoupling from System 1 triggered by involuntary flows from System 1.

Economic Distortions emerge from *decoupling*--when cost and return are separated, or from *cost-return disproportionality*. Perception also can also play a role in altering the cost-return relationship. The *distortions* are typically embodied in human incentives, prices, and the pricing system.

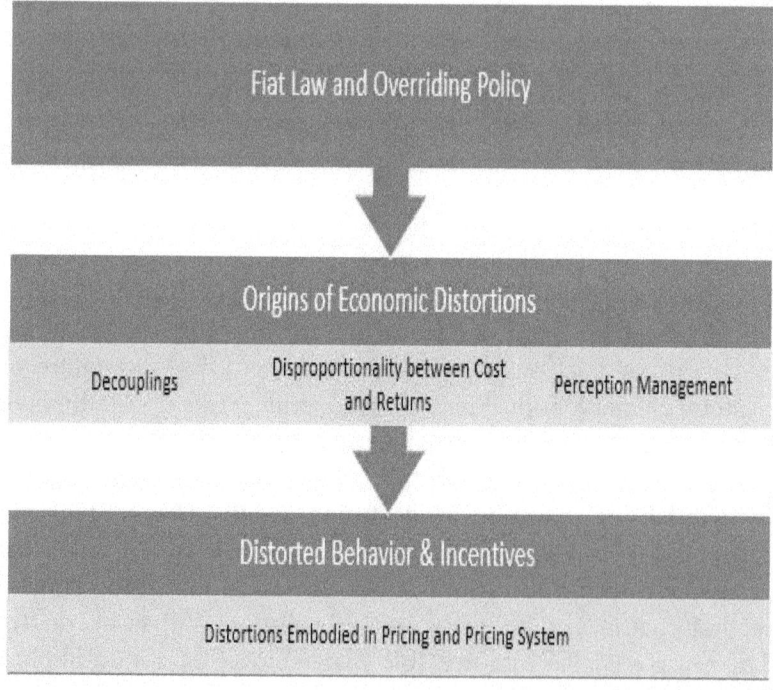

Outcomes. Economic distortions are believed to pose a greater risk of numerous adverse outcomes. The most dangerous potential outcomes are detailed further below after explanation of the abbreviations.

OUTCOMES (Elevated Risk)
- Shortages and Food Crises
- Violence and Death
- Unjust Wealth and Impoverishment
- Oversupply and Waste
- Environmental Damage
- Asset Bubbles and Crashes

Subsystems and Tables
A major element of the model is the policy tables of **System 2**. There are 3 basic subsystems of System 2, each with line-items of major policy interventions. These are:

Subsystem 1 (Sub1): Redistributive (Derivative Inflows and Redistribution with fiat law adjustments; non-fiat financing)

Subsystem 2 (Sub2): Fiat Law: Other Overriding Interventions

Subsystem 3 (Sub3): Fiat Money (Overriding Interventions with Fiat Money Financing; monetary policy with fractional reserve banking)

Columns (all subsystems). Column A through Column E indicate the policies, their scale, rhetorical justification, and the outcome of the decoupling (beneficiaries of wealth gains Column D and cost-bearers Column E). Column F (rent-seeking) through Column M indicate the hypothesized significant events/actions or outcomes within the phases of the feedback loops.

Abbreviations. *Policy interventions* may be abbreviated simply as *interventions* and are presented as line-items and are classified by subsystem and number. For example, **Sub2.5a** means subsystem 2, policy 5a. *Columns* are typically abbreviated "Col" and boldfaced, so that Column D would be written **Col D**.

Most Dangerous Potential Outcomes
In the very first column used for numbering and identifying the policies, a symbol of a circled zero as follows: ⓪ indicates policies that are expected to produce particularly dangerous outcomes such as violence and death (**Sub2.1a, Sub2.2b, Sub2.3a, Sub2.4a, Sub2.4c, Sub2.4d, Sub2.5c, Sub2.6**) food crises/famine (**Sub2.1a, Sub2.2b**), and human rights abuses. A policy that in extreme cases can result in a potentially lethal form of moral hazard observed in *other* outcomes is found in **Sub3.3b** (fiat money as back-up). Two policies are noted that involved environmental damage (**Sub2.5b**) and wildlife (**Sub2.6**).

Where possible, instances where *no official policy* is in effect but an unspoken policy is allowing certain abuses to occur are also noted (e.g. **Sub2.5c**).

Column L (Secondary Impacts following the **Overshoot** phase) suggests several potentially violent outcomes of various policies under the name *crackdowns*.

The problem of *unjust impoverishment* is identified in **Col E** and is present in all subsystems.

Greater Likelihood/Elevated Risk. For **Columns F** through **N**, a digit "1" to indicate a that an activity or outcome of a policy is more *likely*; the "1" is not the probability of an outcome of 1 (100%). The likelihood is left unspecified because of the complexities of nonlinear relationships between variables--the exact outcome of even a single policy is not predictable, let alone the outcome of countless interventions simultaneously interacting, some of which may be removed in some nations while remaining in others. The listing of interventions is neither exhaustive nor definitive; an effort is made to include policies with more significant impacts.

The policy tables employ abbreviations as follows: **Sub1.4a** means **Subsystem 1**, policy 4a; **Sub2.4a Col B** refers to column B of Subsystem 1 policy 4a. Columns are usually abbreviated as **Col.**

Polarity

Two basic systems are posited, simplistically named "System 1" and "System 2." System 1 is titled *economy* and System 2 *derivative inflows*; System 2 acts as an external interventionist force (*interventionism*) into the workings of *economy*, causing economic distortions (i.e. distortions within System 1 *economy*) that result in feedback loops. As will be explained, the *polarity* of System 1 and 2 is *negative* and *positive*, respectively.

Linkage: Fundamental Cost-Return Decoupling

The linkage between the two systems through the process of decoupling is shown here. The arrow at the center shows how System 1 (at right) feeds into System 2 (at left), with negative (-) and positive (+) polarities, respectively. Diagrams of each individual system and their features will be elaborated upon in the next sections.

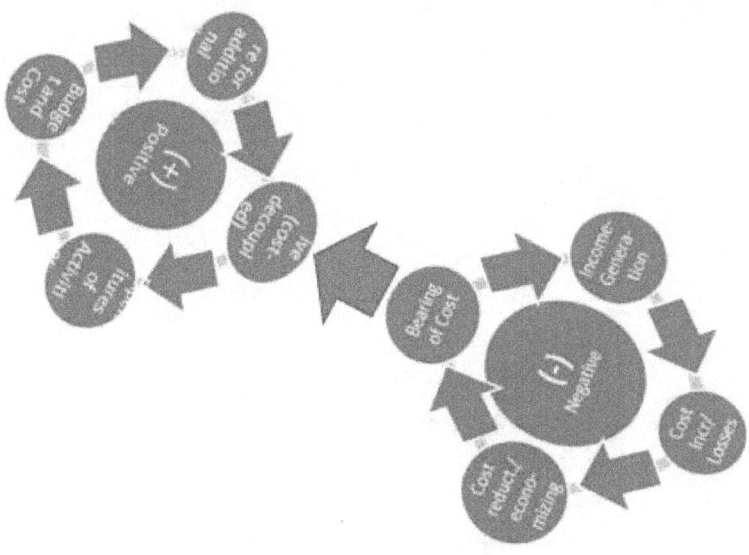

ECONOMY: SYSTEM 1 ARCHITECTURE

System 1's formal name is *economy*. See the table of System 1's basic architecture for details. System 1 may also be abbreviated **Sys1**.

Table of Characteristics and Detail. The basic elements of System 1 are summarized in the table below followed by detailed explanations.

System 1 (Sys1)-Architecture of Economy

Name	Economy
Dominant Goal-Orientation	Economization (=cost reductions) + Voluntary production/selling
Fundamental Relationship(s)	Coupling of return and associated costs; Rates of Return; time units
Financial Entities (Measure of Performance); Principal Actors	
Organizations	Revenues - costs; buyers/sellers/investors
Individuals	Income - cost (of living); buyers/sellers/investors/cared-for
Polarity/Feedback Loop	Negative; Counteracting (e.g. +costs --> -costs)
Dominant Use of Force	Defensive/expulsion; invasive force limited to rescue.
Wealth Accumulation	Compounding of Return(s) over time

Building Block: Fundamental Cost-Return Coupling Bond

The building block of System 1 is posited here: A *cost-return coupling bond* in which *returns* are bound to *cost-bearing*--the *costs borne* to generate that return; this also defines a principle of *ownership* of the return. The reverse is also true: Full ownership of the return implies full ownership of the *costs* associated with that return; in other words, full responsibility, and accountability. A crude representation of the cost-return coupling bond is shown:

Fundamental Coupling Bond

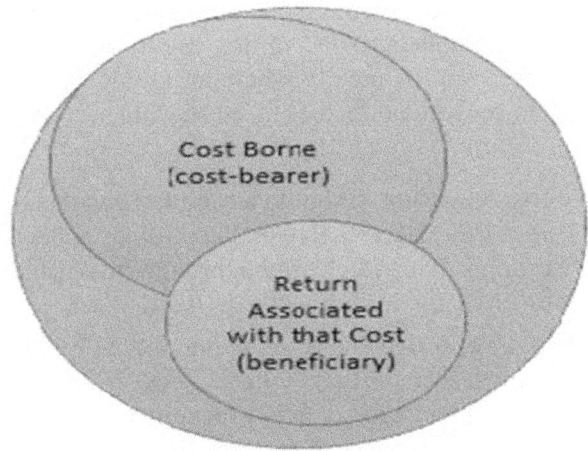

Cost and Return Detail

Within a given time unit, c*ost* is an *outflow/expenditure* (or energy *outflows/expenditure* or *effort*). *Return* is a net *inflow* (or *net* generation of energy-see below). Return can also be negative or zero; there is no assurance of a *positive* return as just noted above.

To summarize, within a *given time unit*:
Positive Return=*Net* Inflow Positive= Inflow less cost >0
Zero Return=*Net* Inflow Zero=Inflow less cost=0
Negative Return=*Net* Inflow Negative=Inflow less cost<0
*Inflow here also means *gross* inflow.

Parallel with Energy. The bond between costs (outflows) and returns (inflows might also be seen from the perspective of energy generation per unit time in the sense that the *return* is a *net inflow* of energy attached to the *energy expenditure (cost)* involved in generating the energy. For example, 1000 joules of energy are generated by some process and the energy use (cost) that is associated with those 1000 joules is 1200 joules, then the *net* inflow is *negative*: 1000-1200= **-200 joules**--a *negative return*.

Interaction Energy and Loss. It is possible that the total energy when cost and return are coupled is greater than when *forcibly* separated (i.e. additional energy/force is required to decouple them), suggesting *greater overall energy use* relative to generation, and therefore an *overall loss* of energy. Any such physical analysis is beyond the scope of this study. Moreover, the point at which fundamental decoupling occurs is ambiguous but is assumed to be approximately where an arrangement becomes *involuntary*, to be detailed further in subsequent sections.

Voluntary Dispossession. It should be emphasized that the owner also may *voluntarily* select to give up the return (net benefit) after receiving/earning it. This can be done through *trade* (in exchange for something else), *gift/donation*, or *destruction*.

The last case--*destruction*—may seem odd, but is relevant in the context of political systems that in theory seek absolutely *equality of result*; this is addressed in the Appendix under the topic of ideology, morality, and political systems.

Proportionality. As noted above, full ownership of the return implies full ownership of the *costs* associated with that return; in other words, full responsibility, and accountability. The return would also be expected to be *proportional*, so that if someone contributes 90% of the cost (which can include *cost in time*), they would be entitled to 90% of any return, unless they agreed otherwise.

Disproportionality. A critical element of economic distortions is cost-return *disproportionality*: Where the full benefit (return) is received while the cost borne is lesser in some proportion (or zero).

Other References to a Coupling Bond Concept

In finance, a clear mathematical description of a coupling bond concept exists: An initial cost *outflow* is linked to future cash (in)flows associated with that cost is seen in *discounted cash flow analysis* (DCF) and in *valuation theory* [Re: *present value, internal rate of return* (IRR); Shim, et al., 1986; Brealey and Myers 1996; Ross, et al. 2008; Damodaran 2012]. *Capitalization theory* also links the cost to the return in some way (Badger 1926, Dewing 1953, Schilt 1982, Pratt 1989).

In physics, for a given energy-generating process, *surplus* energy production (i.e. a positive return) requires that the energy expenditure used* in the process of generating that energy be less than the total energy produced by the process.

**energy expenditure as a measure of cost; surplus energy = total energy produced less energy expended in the process.*

In economics and human action, the concept of *opportunity cost* embodies a coupling bond as well: The "cost" in opportunity cost is what is *lost* by taking an action. If one prefers to take that action voluntarily, there is an implied *return* (what is over and above the *cost* or what is being lost). The opportunity cost does not have to be in monetary terms or in rates of return; it can involve preference in social relationships and countless other scenarios.

A fundamental principle in financial accounting is referred to as the *matching principle*. A key distinction is made between *accrual basis* accounting in which revenues are recognized when earned and costs associated with those revenues are matched to them in the same period; *cash basis* accounting records when cash is received or paid out, which could be during different periods. The *cash flow statement* of a business converts accrual basis to cash basis.

References to some such bond in other disciplines are likely to exist. However, two others that may apply (depending on the proper interpretation) are described briefly here.

1. **Scripture**. Remarkably, a reference in *Genesis*: 3 suggests a coupling bond. Reliance solely upon the production (fruit) of Divine Providence is not enough to provide for a growing population. Therefore, what must humanity do? The tree of knowledge of good and evil (from which Eve ate and gave some to her husband) teaches us that if we bear children and multiply our numbers we cannot support *ourselves by just picking fruit*— in other words, *enjoying the fruit (return) without bearing any cost* is the path to death ("...or you shall die." 3.3). Therefore, agricultural production (bearing a cost to produce food or "...to till the ground..." 3.23) is fundamental. With this knowledge,

Adam joins God ("becomes like one of us, knowing good and evil" 3.22) and takes from the *tree of life* (producing enough to feed a growing family/population) to "…eat and live forever" (3.22). To live forever also suggests economic sustainability. (Oxford University Press (Bible) 2001)

2. Concept of (No) Skin in the Game

Full accountability means that the *costs* of our actions are fully recognized and felt by us, including financially. It follows that any returns/net benefits that result from one's actions should embody full accountability –*connection to the full cost of those actions*. Those in society who can reap rewards (return) without having to bear any cost (no "skin in the game") are in a unique position that could be described in the best terms as truly fortuitous, and in worse terms as dangerous, depending upon the those who have this capability, and implications for policy actions (See Taleb 2012 and 2016b; concepts of *antifragility, precautionary principle*).

Quoting from scripture above should not be interpreted as promoting a religion, but rather as an attempt to identify a possible *moral principle* based on the concept of a coupling bond as a basis for social justice. Although initially appearing as irrelevant to policy, this is an important point because of the history of *rhetorical justifications* for policy interventions based on fairness and morality (**Col C**).

System Features

System 1 (economy) combines two activities on the foundation of the coupling bond from above: Economization and voluntary production/selling.

1. Economization

Economization is often expressed through *cost savings*, minimization of *outflows*, *price competition*, *lower costs*, and *miniaturization*—in terms of less space usage). *Time* is a precious resource and the economization of *time* is fundamental (=ability to produce in less time; time-saving).

2. Voluntary Production and Selling. Producing and/or selling to meet the voluntary demand of *buyers* (consumers; businesses purchasing goods, inputs, or labor) through exchange at some agreed-upon price: In other words, price as an *exchange rate* between good x and good y. ("One can purchase with what one has produced;" Re: Say's Law; Say 1803, Sowell 1973, Hutt 1974; note that a pervasive error describing Say's law is: "supply creates its own demand;" Klein 1983).

The price can be *zero* as productive activities can be sold for *nothing*, to be detailed further later). Productive activities can also be *services*, including the provision/supply of information.

The combination of (1) and (2) may produce a *positive return* for the producer; some actors of the system may be content with a *zero return*, although many may tend to strive for a *positive return* if possible. A positive return is not guaranteed and is subject to a variety of factors including market conditions, character and values, skill sets including management, technical, and entrepreneurial foresight. Misinformation and economic distortions also play a key role in returns, also to be detailed later. For an organization, the economization process is typically measured as: *revenues less costs*; for individuals, *income less cost (of living)*.

Accounting for Economization and Selling

Net Benefit (Returns) Accounting

Net benefit accounting is, for *a given unit of time*:

Revenues (or *income* for individuals)
Less: **Costs** (resources expended or consumed)
= **Return**

Revenues (inflows) may tend to rise the more customer needs are met, while **costs (outflows)** decline when the organization economizes on its use of resources.

Return. The difference between the two (revenues less cost) is the *return* (also called *net benefit*, which means benefit net of *cost*). In cashflow financial terms, a positive return can also be referred to as *positive net cash flow*.

Return and Cost within the Coupling Bond
Also called *net* benefit, net income, profit*[1], *or saved income*[2]; return is a *flow* in each unit of time, which if positive, is a measure of *increase* in *wealth*; in physical terms, this could be described as an increase in net energy units generated (e.g. joules).
**The word "net" typically means net of costs associated with generating the return (net benefit).*
[1] **Profit.** The term profit may be misleading in that it appears to be *stand-alone* as if a benefit is received (the profit) with *no cost or input attached to it.* The term "return" viewed as reflecting the reality more clearly because it emphasizes a return *on a cost borne (cost-bearing)* – referring to the underlying coupling bond which is the *fundamental association of the return with the costs incurred to generate that return*.
Note that in historical *policy formulation* there can be a moral and ideological basis in *profit* as being fundamentally *evil* or *immoral*; this is used as justification for taking it away from the cost-bearers (to be redistributed, or in extreme cases, destroyed). This policy-based element of the model is partly addressed in the Appendix (Ideology, Morality, and Political Systems).

Justice and Origins of Cost Avoidance. A crucial source of confusion also lies in the absence of accounting for *costs* of actions—for instance, a business or unscrupulous individual that *avoids bearing the full costs of their actions*, while receiving the *full* benefit associated with that (partially avoided) cost would be considered unjustifiable. Here, cost-return disproportionality applies and *the origins of cost avoidance* must be investigated (this is addressed in **Sub2.5b** and **Sub2.5c** –cost transfers and judicial immunity)

²Saved income: Return is a *flow "saved"* in the sense of being an *excess* over the cost. *Saved income* is distinct from the term "savings" which is a *stock* at a *given point of time*, including as a *store of value*; savings are an accumulated stock of one or more *individual* positive returns over time. In the section below on wealth accumulation and compounding, resources for *investing* draw from:
(1) savings or stores of value accumulated beforehand;
(2) positive returns (accumulated in the same period).

Perspectives on Economization
The importance of economization cannot be underestimated. Some other aspects are discussed here as well as in illustrations in the Appendix.
Deflation and Increased Purchasing Power. Through economization, as price declines continue over time, *economy* is inherently deflationary. When prices decline, *purchasing power* increases, so that there is a compounding effect of purchasing power over time (on *deflation* see Borio, et al. 2015).
Remarkably, an increase in purchasing power is a form of increased income and wealth (for details, see Kennedy (2016): 47-50). Therefore, with deflation, *cash/currency* that one holds today--*if there is no future inflation (dilution of currency by additional fiat money creation)* --can be more valuable in the future. Because in our modern monetary system (20th-early 21st century) we are accustomed to inflation, this is not immediately obvious. Nor should it be assumed that in the future we can expect to see a deflationary economic environment. The norm now in history is inflation as seen in Subsystem 3: fiat money. [Re: "shrinkflation" in which prices (invisibly) rise through shrinking package contents and sizes].
A distinction should be made between deflation in terms of increased purchasing power and *balance sheet* (or *asset*) deflation. The latter hurts debtors who have collateralized their debts with assets that are deflating in value. Typically, criticisms of deflation will refer to this form of hardship for debtors (whether individuals

and firms). Because of the policy-based debt-bias of the economy, deflating assets values can be devastating for borrowers (Re: negative home equity; Stockman 2013).

Human Ingenuity and Economization of Time (Cost in Time). Generally invisible in this growth dynamic but equally critical to compounding is *time embodied within rates of return*. Time is a *limited* and *irreplaceable* resource for humans, and finding ways to use time itself wisely can be easily forgotten: This valuable freed-up time can be used to innovate to increase future positive return(s) in time. This requires creative thought and problem-solving combined with inventive manipulation of physical things/engineering, mechanical and other skills; managerial and selling abilities also are essential components of this process.

Rates of Return

The term *rate of return*, is *not* the return itself, but a *ratio* of return to cost in the *same* period as follows:

$$\text{Return/Cost.}$$

This simple rate of return designation is specifically termed *rate of return on cost* (RRC) as detailed in Kennedy (2016).

The RRC can also be thought of as a fundamental ratio of net inflows (or net energy generation) relative to outflows/expenditures (or energy *outflows/expenditure*) in the same time unit, typically expressed in (physical) cash flows.

From above, reducing cost in time relates to *rate of return*. If the *same* return can be achieved in less time, the rate of return increases for the given time period: For example, in year 1 a business has a return of 100 (e.g. Revenue of 1600 less cost of 1500) over that year (=12 months). By the net benefit accounting from above, the rate of return is return/cost (=100/1500) or about 6.7%. In year 2, assume that the business is now operating at lower cost such that a return of 100 is attained in only 92% of the time (about 11 months). This implies that the (annualized) rate of return of the company has increased by 1/12 or by about 8% over year 1.

Assuming annual revenues unchanged at 1600 and a cost decline to 1492, the return is 108 and the annual rate of return is (=108/1492) to about 7.2%.

Of course, it is usually more clear and practical to simply wait until the end of year 2 to confirm that the return increased by 8% over year 1 (from 100 to 108), since everything is measured in time constants, but the importance of time as a resource--and *time use as an investment*--is essential.

An example of rate of return as measured by the RRC is shown with financial data of a consumer goods firm in the form of a *relative frequency distribution*:

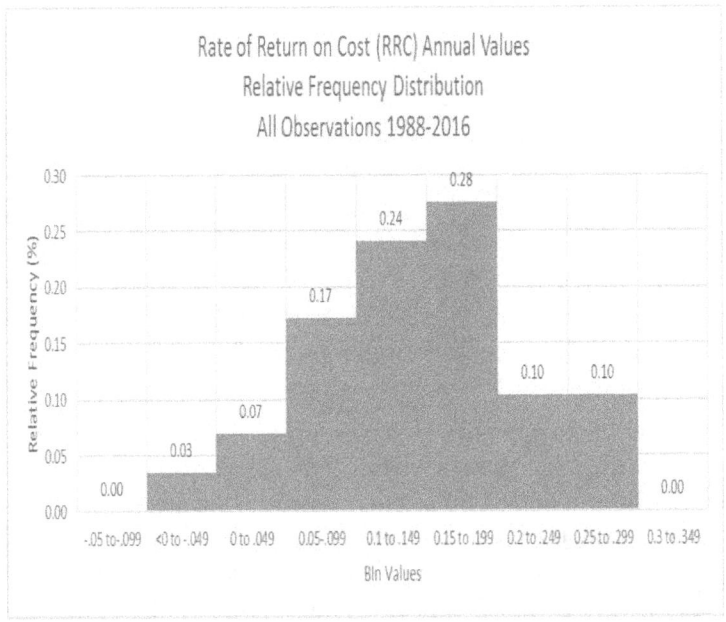

The distribution above spans almost three decades, the rate of return can vary considerably. Therefore, businesses can see elevated rates of return for some periods, followed by declines to zero and even *negative* rates of return (the same logic can apply to individuals).

The Threat of AI and Economization. A widespread concern is the advance of AI (*artificial intelligence*) combined with automation and robotics leading to the relentless replacement of humans in the workplace. It is feared that without employment, humans will be unable to purchase even the most basic goods and the very survival of humanity could be at stake. The economic reasoning should consider not only the ability to *purchase*, but also the ability to *sell*. If firms employing robots instead of humans are unable to produce goods that are *affordable* for potential buyers (including the replaced/displaced workers), they will be unable to sell their goods and will fail financially. The result will be both destitute displaced workers *and* bankrupt companies trying to sell overpriced goods to them. In sum, firms adopting AI, robots, and automation to reduce costs will be self-sustaining only if they can survive by selling at affordable prices *and* earning a positive return from doing so. Not all suppliers/producers will succeed in managing this difficult process.

Nevertheless, preparing for a future with evolving definitions of work and alternative streams of income and sources and ideas for wealth creation is essential. (Rifkin 1996; Sethi 2009; Diamandis 2014; Thiel 2014; Altucher 2015; Smith 2015; Ferriss 2016; also Re: *universal basic income*; Bregman 2017).

Variations in Propensity to Economize. There is no imperative to economize, other than hopefully to cover one's costs and have some cushion for hard times. Some people prefer to save, others less so. Some businesses are successful at reducing costs and raising returns, others are not; bankruptcy is possible for entities that have taken on too much debt to finance operations and can no longer repay the loan(s). Certain organizations that do not have owner-investors may seek at minimum to cover costs. Some for-profit businesses, including some family businesses, may choose to operate closer to breakeven rather than to maximize returns. While in some cases tax-planning is the motivation to reduce net income, there are cases where the short-term current maximization of income or returns is less vital than maintaining loyalty with customers for long-term business prospects.

There are actors/entities in System 1 that do not necessarily earn income from current activities, such as retirees or investment organizations who rely upon income generated from invested assets (invested from previous savings). Individuals unable to care for themselves may depend upon family friends, church and community or System 2 entities (Re: **Sub1.1**) to cover all or part of their living costs. Organizations that are either start-ups or that are ongoing entities but that are unable to cover their costs from revenue (inflows) may seek financing to fund the shortfall by raising capital through borrowing (debt) or issuing shares (equity; Re: initial public offerings; IPOs).

Qualifications and Clarifications

It is not necessarily the case that economization and meeting buyer demand will always be successful. There is no guarantee that revenues will always remain above costs; many businesses and households struggle to cover costs and face financial hardship despite their best efforts. **Economic distortions** also are thought to play a serious role in individual hardships, financial crises, and bank failures, as will be explored in the section on System 2.

Individuals/Households. For individuals or households, the term *income* is used rather than revenues. Reducing one's expenses is a form of economizing: In the case of individuals, living expenses is usually referred to as the *cost of living*. Income minus the cost of living is the amount saved each month (also called a net benefit or return). The saved amount (saved income) in that time period is a *flow*, which is distinct from the word "savings" which is an accumulation or *stock* of saved income; saved income in each period is added together to build up savings.

Money Optional vs. Practical. Physical money does not necessarily need to be involved in System 1, although some means of payment, which can include food items, obligations of other parties to return favors, etc., is needed for individuals or businesses to cover costs. Where perishable goods or less durable stores of value are concerned, some type of money might be preferable due to short shelf life.

Sustainability and Future Trends. Because of the self-correcting counterbalancing feedback loop of System 1, on a larger scale System 1 may tend to be more sustainable, although many individual returns (individuals and businesses) may often be negative in the process.

The system is viewed as more sustainable because of the counterbalancing feedback loop that allows the system to "correct" by *economizing* when costs are rising and resources are being overused. The mechanism that signals overuse is *pricing*, to be detailed further below and in Appendix 1.

A long-term outcome of System 1 not noted in the table above is believed to be *miniaturization* (economization by using *less space*), and a form of *decentralization* of which the dominant feature is *decentralized information* due in part to the lowering costs of information and leading to the ability to engage in productive activity from multiple locations rather than one centralized location (Re: The Internet; digital technologies; 3-D printing, etc.)

On decentralization in a historical context, see Barzun (2001) and Van Creveld (1999). *The Law of Accelerating Returns* (Kurzweil 2001) concerns the cost reductions of both information and the production of technologies as the return continues to rise in terms of faster microchip speeds.

Wealth Accumulation via Compounding: System 1

After a positive return can be generated, investing that amount allows the wealth to accumulate through *compounding*. Counterintuitively, this accumulation embodies *economization* (declining costs) that figures into the rate of return.

Future Orientation (Future Value). Wealth accumulation is *future-oriented*. The formula for future wealth accumulation (*future value*) with *continuous* compounding is:

$$W_t = C_0 e^{rt}$$

The formula can be seen from more than one perspective, but the aim is the same: To reap a future *return* from an initial (current) *outflow* of resources. *Money* does not necessarily have to be involved; the expansion in wealth could be fish, acorns, joules of energy stored in our bodies, or even social credits with friends, family, and community, but quantification is made somewhat easier with financial data.

The variable C is *cost* (cost as an *outflow* or *resources given up, invested,* or *sacrificed* in exchange for a hope-for future return). Where the C_0 comes from is rarely addressed, but is either stored reserves (*positive return* that was generated *previously* and stored/saved up), or from a *current*-period positive return.

The variable W is the future value of that initial outflow (C), or the wealth accumulated at the end of *t* periods.

The Future Return (Net Benefit). The difference between W_t and C_0 is the wealth *increase* over that time which is the *return, net benefit,* or *profit* of that initial investment over time.

The variable *r*: Rate of Return
What future interest rate *r* should be used? Since the future is not known, forecasts are made. When computing expected rates of return, it is most common to forecast of a stream of future net cash flows (NCF) over a certain number of periods *n*. The *internal rate of return* (IRR) is the rate of return at which these forecasted *net cash flows* (also referred to here as *cash returns*) *exactly* equal the amount of the initial investment outflow (C_0).

Solving for *r* we obtain the *internal rate of return* (IRR):

$$NCF_1/(1+r) + NCF_2/(1+r^2) + \ldots + NCF_n/(1+r^n) = C_0$$

Often the *net* cash flows (NCF) are simply abbreviated as "cash flows," but the *net* (as in net of cost) should be clarified.

Economization embodied in *r*: Net Cash Flows. It should be emphasized *economization* plays a central role in the future rate of return: Forecasted net cash flows (NCF) can be expected to rise as costs of a business are reduced relative to revenues. Therefore, the business itself increases its *own* future value through economization and positive returns year after year.

Economization embodied in *r*: Cost Reductions. A critical point is that the IRR can also be computed based not only on forecasted net cash flows as above, but as *future savings* and *future purchasing power* (Kennedy 2016: 47-50).

The scenarios are noted here:

1. **Future savings** (=reduction in costs and future cash *outflows*) are generated from making an investment (e.g. a solar power unit). In this case, the future cash flows are *reductions* in *outflows* (i.e. amounts saved) because of lowered costs.

2. **Future purchasing power** of the asset. Two cases must be examined as one relates to (a) economization; and the other (b) asset appreciation, which may be caused by certain economic distortions, or may be related to economization.

(a) **Cash/currency and Economy-wide Cost Reductions.** Remarkably, and often unnoticed because increased purchasing power from *deflation* is not a common feature of our modern economic system, cash/currency itself can be viewed as the initial investment C_0. As prices of goods and services decline (=decline in cost of living) due to an overall economy-wide ability of producers to sustainably reduce their costs, purchasing power rises and the value of the cash increases (appreciation).

(b) **Asset Appreciation (Non-cash/non-currency assets).** Purchasing power increases when a non-*cash* asset appreciates in value relative to the *cost of living* (or relative to the value of other assets). Examples of assets are countless, but can include stocks, bonds (see note on bonds below), real estate, precious metals, and collectibles; in recent years *fiat crypto-assets* such as *bitcoin* (covered in Sub**3.6b**) may have restrictive monetary policies that limit supply relative to demand, pushing up the value.

Analysis of (b): Economization or Other Drivers of Appreciation. It is essential to clarify that the appreciation in the value of the assets in (b) above is *not necessarily related to economization*. Fiat money, the extension of credit and increased demand (relative to supply) for various reasons are potentially dominant forces in such asset appreciation. For details on *economic distortions* see the relevant discussions.

Where economization is more likely to relate to *asset appreciation* is when a company can (or expected to) realize cost savings. This can occur from general cost-cutting measures or through *merger and acquisition* (M&A) where cost redundancies are eliminated between the entities. In some cases, *spin-offs* may also be expected to generate efficiencies and cost savings, as well.

*Note on bonds: Unless bonds are *variable-interest*, the interest they pay is *fixed* (Re: *fixed income*). For fixed-income, differences arise between the rate paid on the bond (coupon) and the *yield to maturity* (YTM) on the bond. The YTM can be significantly influenced by policy interest rates (see Subsystem 3 and **Sub3.1**).

In a zero or near-zero policy interest rate environment, how can investor earn a return? Bonds still can generate *capital gains* when central bank buying pushes up bond prices (due to the inverse relationship between bond prices and yields, this lowers the yield— even into negative interest rates); other sources of capital gains can be short-term bond trading activity, or when investors regard bonds as a *safe haven asset* and bid up their price (e.g. in the event of a stock market crash). Note however, that *inflation risk* of bonds remains a concern if the purchasing power of the original face value of the bond at maturity is significantly reduced.

Underlying Source of Return. How does the business's *own* returns and rates of return relate to the rate of return on the investment for the investor in the example above? Because as returns rise for firms themselves, they can increase the *dividends* they can pay out. What if no dividends are paid? Even if the firm doesn't pay dividends, the return exists as *equity income* *attributable to investors* (Kennedy 2014) or, for debt instruments, the *interest rate* that they can pay (e.g. bonds).

Compounding and the term *e* is the universal growth constant equal approximately to 2.7128... (Re: Euler's number). The constant *e* is used to generate a result with *continuous* compounding, meaning that any amount earned instantaneously begins to earn more *on top of itself*, repeated continuously. (Side note: A remarkable property of Euler's number is that the *increase in wealth (return)* grows at the same rate as the *rate of return*.)

(For a historical financial application in the oil and gas industry, Re: Hotelling principle; Hotelling 1931; Devajaran 1981; Miller and Upton 1985; Klein 1983 regarding theoretical equalization of rates of return on assets).

Other Compounding Periods
Continuous compounding above does not necessarily apply to securities and financial instruments that may have compounding periods that differ. The formula to specify the number of compounding periods *t* varies from the one above as follows:

$$W_t = C_0(1+r)^t$$

Wealth-Building in a Financial Instrument Context. In the context of investing, the rate of return *r* varies according to the asset invested in. For example, the rate of return on a certificate of deposit (CD) or interest-bearing savings account is its *interest rate*, for a bond it is the *yield*, * and for a stock is often based on the *total return* which combines dividends paid* and capital appreciation of the stock.

Notes:
1. The *yield* (*yield to maturity* or YTM) of the bond is also the IRR.
2. Two points regarding dividends: (a) *Dividend growth*. A stock that *grows* its dividend annually generates a higher rate of return

(as computed by the IRR) than one that does not grow its dividend (Re: *dividend aristocrats, dividend achievers*; Lichtenfeld 2015; Peters 2008, 2016). (b) *Initial dividend yield*: Assuming two stocks each with zero capital appreciation in the future. The stock with a *high initial dividend yield even with zero dividend growth --if it sustains its dividend payments over an extended period*--can generate a higher rate of return than a stock with a *low initial dividend yield* and high dividend growth.

Compounding varies according to the investment: Bonds often pay twice annually (semi-annual coupons); dividends, if paid, are typically paid quarterly (4 times/year). For a bank certificate of deposit (CD) *daily or monthly* may be advertised. The *annual percentage yield* (APY) is computed based on the frequency of compounding and the interest rate (Re: CD calculators; Bankrate)

Computing Return and Rate of Return. From above, the *return* is the difference between the *future value* W_t and the *initial cost/outflow* (W_t-C_0). The *return* and *rate of return* can be computed if the W_t is assumed to be a particular value in the future. For example, if W_t is 110 and C_0 is 100, with $t=1$ (a single time period such as 1 year), then the *return* is W_t -C_0 or 110-100=10 and the annual *rate of return* is computed as either: (10 /100) or (110/100)-1) which is 0.10 (or 10% per year). For more than one time period, assuming the same data as before and 10 periods, the annual rate of return is computed as follows: $(110/100)^{(1/10)}$ which is just under 1%.

Alternative scenarios involving wealth accumulation and compound growth are provided in Appendix 3, including varying rates of return, destruction of wealth, no (apparent) resources to invest with, and accounting for the impact of taxes and inflation on wealth accumulation.

Other Clarifications

Cash Flow Emphasis. Note that the variables are represented by *cash flows* (cash flows *in* and cash flows *out*) due to cash's physical and financial nature.

Ethics and Wealth Accumulation. A criticism of wealth accumulation is that solely focusing on maximizing rates of return is wrong if business practices of firms being invested in are unethical. This is a key point that relates to the concept of *cost-bearing* and the coupling bond: The *cost* must be fully felt by the (business) entity receiving the benefit and should not be transferred to others; otherwise, firms have an unfair advantage and someone else is being harmed—this exemplifies the central problem of policy-originated *economic distortions* of this book.

If the critical issue of *cost-bearing* is properly addressed, then the question becomes whether it is moral to allow people to accumulate wealth. Wealth obtained can be used for good, not only in the form of *philanthropy* and *charitable giving*, but also to encourage entrepreneurial activity and job creation towards solving problems and fulfilling human needs, including humanity's major challenges (Sethi 2009; Diamandis 2014; Thiel 2014; Gates 2017; Small 2017 (Re: Melinda Gates). Also refer to *venture capital*, *angel investing*, *crowdfunding*, *business incubators* (e.g. Idealab); *microbusinesses, start-ups*.

With regards to charitable and volunteer organizations (non-profits (NPOs), churches, etc.), many may rely on highly variable *voluntary donations* or *memberships* as a principal source of their revenues/income. Their efforts play an important role in a wide variety of highly worthy causes including food and medical aid, human and animal rights, among many other causes. Some organizations may rely on a mix of voluntary funding and taxpayer funds. Many such organizations might rely upon fund *accounting* to maintain a balance between inflows and outflows/costs as part of their financial management.

Ethical issues are also discussed in the Appendix on the topic of ideology, morality, and political systems as well as in wealth accumulation scenarios.

System 1 Use of Force
When there are problems involving safety of person or property and other means are not possible, a critical question is what kind of force is appropriate. In System 1, it is assumed that the dominant form is *defensive* force and self-protection, keeping out/repelling intruders or expelling certain individuals from the organization. Defensive force can be implemented by hiring some form of security forces for protection. *Expulsion* is another form of defensive force in the sense of removing individuals from the organization who fail to conform to the organizational guidelines (internal policies or code of conduct; also see Policies in System 1 in the next section below).
If *invasive* force is used (e.g. forced entry onto private property or physically restraining someone), its justification might be for some form of rescue effort or protection of someone else against an aggressor.
Force in not considered justified to separate (decouple) returns from their associated costs (decoupling); those who bear the costs are innately assumed to be the beneficiaries of and be the owners of what those costs return.

The issue of force (coercion) is central because the involuntary portion of System 2's interventions into System 1 are considered justified based on fairness and need, and to rectify injustices. This will be discussed further in the section on rhetorical justifications (**Col C**) and in the Appendix.

Policies in System 1
System 1 entities such as private businesses also have *internal policies* and *codes of conduct*. The primary difference is that failure to abide by these policies tends to result in enforcement via *expulsion* from the organization. If the action involves certain rules for which enforcement is legally administered by authorities outside of the organization such as against *theft* or *embezzlement*, then in addition to expulsion the suspected party will be referred

to the court system (typically administered by Sys2's authorities for processing).

Another dimension of policy in System 1 involves *codification* of rules for master-planned communities or other types of contractual communities: C, C&Rs (Codes, Covenants, and Restrictions), or the legal codes governing mobile home and RV parks. For enforcement purposes, these rules may be embodied in the laws of the jurisdiction in which they reside (e.g. state or national laws, etc.). (Also see Hahm 2017; *agrihoods*-- agriculture-centered master-planned communities).

System 1 Polarity and Feedback Loop

System 1's dominant polarity is *negative*, described by a *counteracting* feedback loop. What this means is that when costs for a financial entity begin to rise, there is a tendency for the entity to counteract this occurrence by seeking ways to reduce costs. Therefore, rising costs will tend to be followed by some movement towards reducing those costs. However, the efforts to reduce costs may not always be successful as keeping costs under control requires managerial skills.

The long-term tendency of this counteracting feedback loop is the lowering not only of costs for the entities themselves, but of prices of goods and services. This counteracting feedback loop also tends to come into conflict with the feedback loop of System 2, to be seen later.

The feedback loop and polarity of System 1 are shown here:

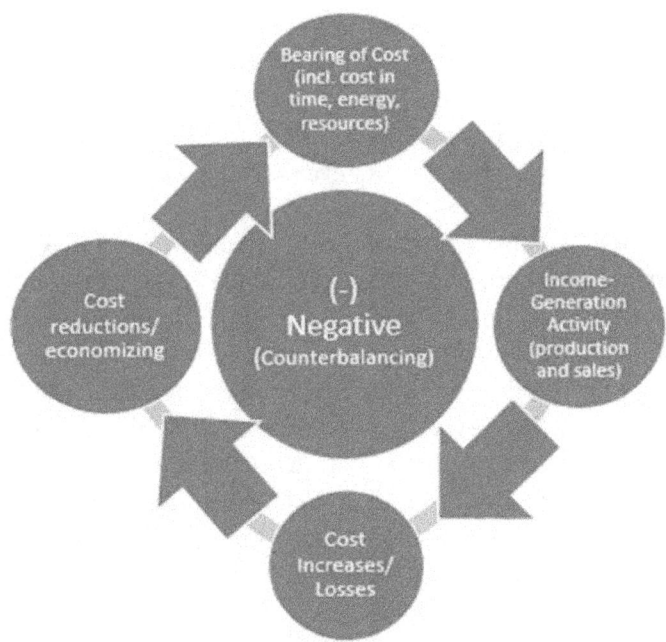

Linkages: System 1 to System 2 Decoupling Process

Recall that in System 1, the fundamental relationship assumes that the *return* (also called *net benefit* =benefit after costs) accrues to the entity that incurs the cost, unless this right is *voluntarily* given away (by donation, grant, etc.)

In the table of System 1's architecture, the line item "taxes, fines, and fees" is the link from System 1 to System 2 which involves a *decoupling of potential return* for System 1 entities; in other words, had the entities retained this amount, their returns relative to costs would have been higher. In physical terms, this also suggests an *energy loss* within System 1 when the decoupling becomes involuntary, to be further discussed below.

The term "taxation" is most commonly used to describe this decoupling process, but a definitional issue plus two assumed components need to be addressed:

Income-based Fees and Components. *Taxes* as they are traditionally referred to are thought of here as *fees based on some measure of income*; and are a primary *decoupling intervention* (to be discussed below). The income of financial entities upon which the fees are based include *gross revenues, net income*, or *wage income*.

Property taxes (such as land or taxes on real estate) may not appear to be an income-based tax, but since assessed value of properties ultimately tend to be related to incomes in that area (i.e. high-income earners tend to be able to purchase more expensive properties), they might also be included as income-based. As for certain *punitive fines and/or penalties** that typically target businesses for legal/regulatory violations such as *antitrust laws,* * they may not appear to be directly income-based either but it may be that *larger* financial entities (in terms of *business revenues* and geographic scope) might tend to be the target of *larger* penalties than smaller entities.

Therefore, overall the fees we call "taxes", as well as certain fines are broadly categorized as "income-based fees."

***Notes**: *Certain fines such as parking (meter) violations are not considered to be applicable here since the amounts tend to be fixed rather than based on the income of the offender.*
Regarding antitrust laws of the U.S., refer to the Sherman Antitrust Act (1890), Clayton Act and Federal Trade Commission Act (both 1914).

Principal/Agent Problem and Incentives. Fees are initially assumed to be paid in exchange for a service. However, a complicated element of income-based fees is the existence of two assumed basic components arising from a *principal/agent problem*. Briefly stated an agency problem is said to exist when someone is expected to act on behalf of someone else's interest: "…the incentives between the agent and the principal are not perfectly aligned and conflicts of interest arise. As a result, the agent may be tempted to act in his or her own interest rather than (sic) the principal's." (Financial Times, 2017) (Re: Agency theory; Fama and Jensen 1983; Eisenhardt 1989)

In this case, the *principal* is the income-based fee payer (taxpayer) and the *agent* is the responsible party(ies) for providing what is very broadly called *public services** at various administrative and jurisdictional levels (township, city, county/parish, state/province, national, etc.).

1. Commensurate/Voluntary: A portion of the income-based inflows may be considered reasonable for the services being provided to System 1; these are referred to as *commensurate/voluntary* because their cost is perceived as essentially no different than if the services were provided by and within System 1. If the *services** provided by System 2 are charged at the same rate as if they had been provided by and within System 1 alone; this commensurate amount is *voluntary*--the essential basis of *economy* (System 1) (Also see Walker 1888 regarding *involuntary* activity as *non-economic*). In this sense, this portion of any such fees could be viewed as remaining within System 1.

*Note: Public Services/Services. Many of these services are also provided in some form within the framework of System 1; when the services are "bought" through income-based fees, as traditionally has been the case, these can be referred to as *public services,* provided at various administrative levels. The definition of *essential* public services varies, but can include provision of security (law enforcement), social services, justice, code enforcement, sanitation and drainage, roads, bridges, and other infrastructure.

2. Decoupling of Return and Associated Cost: Involuntary. An amount that is paid (cost) that is perceived to *exceed* what is reasonable in exchange for the service (the return). Essentially, the buyers of the services at some point become *involuntary*. Once this occurs, for the continuation of the arrangement, some level of coercion or the threat of coercion may be applied.

However, due to the innate reinforcing feedback loop associated with a derivative inflow structure, over time the fees associated with the services are expected to move *upwards* more likely than downwards; the income-based fees may at a certain point be viewed as *exceeding* the voluntary *subjective value* of the *income-based fee payers* (more generally referred to as *taxpayers*) but also abbreviated here as *income-based payers*. **Qualification**. With regards to smaller communities, city-states and even nations with smaller populations and a higher population density it could be somewhat more likely that the income-based fees will remain voluntary for *longer* due to proximity-based local responsiveness on the part of System 2 actors at that smaller scale.

This is the origin of the decoupling that gives rise to divergent polarities described by two dominant feedback loops: The dominant *reinforcing* feedback loop of System 2, and simultaneously an assumed additional *counterbalancing* feedback loop from System 1 that can adversely affect incentives to produce and earn income (to lower the cost –of the fees).
This disincentive effect also implies a theorized *loss of energy* to the system.
This initial distortion is the first in a possible series of additional distortions as seen in subsequent interventions found in System 2's subsystems, and phases; while elevated risks of occurrence are posted, the highly complex non-linear interactions between these may render estimation of the likelihood of outcomes difficult.

Uncertainty and Insecurity. For System 1 entities, a complication and source of confusion regarding income-based fees is their potential for *ambiguity*. The final amount owed is not necessarily known until after the calendar (or fiscal) year has ended and the full amount of the income is known and computed. Meanwhile, System 2's policies can change regarding how much is to be paid based on income. This can complicate the decision-making process for System 1 entities and contributes to a problem of *insecure ownership* highlighted in the discussion on Sys2 subsystems.

Comparative Polarity and Feedback Loops

Both components of income-based fees are subject to System 1's *counteracting (or counterbalancing) feedback loop* towards cost reductions, so that System 1's entities move to lower this type of cost (i.e. economization in time and resources).

In contrast, the dominant feedback loop of System 2 is a *reinforcing (positive)*. This reinforcing impact can over time lead to *overreach* and tend to inflate the fees beyond what System 1 may deem justified, setting in motion other feedback loops to be discussed. This feedback loop will be seen in the discussion regarding System 2.

The long-term *interaction* between the two feedback loops is expected to result in problems occurring in *overshoot* and *reversal* (or possibly collapse) phases to be discussed. An *intermediate S-curve* pattern may also be a possible outcome.

The interaction of both systems is shown below again, from the overview. The feedback loop and polarity diagram for System 2 is shown separately in the section detailing System 2 Architecture.

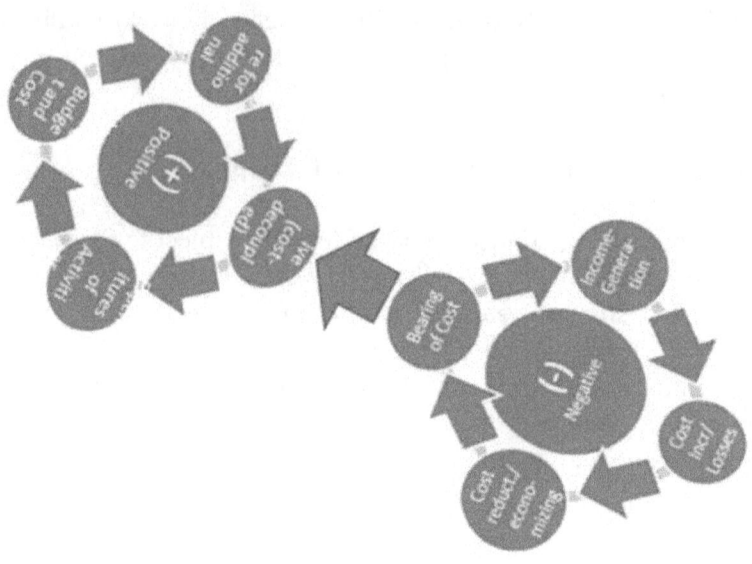

Derivative Inflows to System 2: Overview

The central arrow in the diagram above indicates the linkage and derivative inflows from System 1 (lower right) to System 2 (upper left).

Concept of Cost. With a derivative inflow structure, the inflows into System 2 are used for various purposes broadly termed *expenditures*, but the key point is that in System 2 the concept of *cost* in the same sense as in System 1 is not relevant because the costs are borne in System 1.

Rent-Seeking (Col F). Derivative inflows into System 2 indicated by the central arrow above into System 2 are directed according to various priorities; entities engage in *rent-seeking* to have the flows directed towards them. *Elected officials*, *lawmakers* or *politicians* have the power to provide benefits in exchange for political support (e.g. election). The process of exchanging votes for benefits can help direct funds or give preferential treatment towards the supporters (such as *special interest groups*). In subsystem 1, the favors are *redistribution* policies (without the fiat money element).

Overrides (Fiat Law). Funds into System 2 enable fiat law overrides, through *legislation/lawmaking* in some cases, by *executive order*. These overrides may involve the redirection of funds, as well. *Fiat law* accords *redistributive* (Subsystem 1) or *regulatory/legal* (Subsystem 2) privileges than can override previous laws and agreements-- over the voluntary *decisions of others* including consumers and parties in contractual arrangements. (Bastiat 1850; Benson 2011).

The overrides can include *extra-judicial* actions such that the courts and justice system are bypassed to determine guilt or innocence, noted particularly in **Col L**.

In Subsystem 3, the focus is on the monetary and financial overrides that can deliver benefits with the aid of fiat money.

DERIVATIVE INFLOWS: SYSTEM 2 ARCHITECTURE

Table of Characteristics and Detail. The following is a table of major features of System 2. System 2 may also be abbreviated Sys2.

System 2 (Sys2)-Derivative, Decoupled Inflows

Name	Derivative Inflows
Dominant Goal-Orientation	Inflow Maximization (See Subsystems)
Fundamental Relationship(s)	Derived Inflows=>Sys2 Expenditures
Financial Entities (Measure of Performance)	
Organizations + Individuals	Derivative Inflows; Rent-seeking
Polarity/Feedback Loop	Positive; Reinforcing (e.g. +inflows--> +inflows)
Dominant Use of Force	Defensive/expulsion; Invasive (Various forms)
Wealth Accumulation	Derivative Inflows

System 2's more formal name is *derivative inflows*. The term "inflows" is used because the funds that come into System 2 are derived from either System 1, or from fiat money sources of

System 2 Subsystem 3 (to be detailed further below). These inflows are cost-decoupled, and therefore are costless or low-cost funding to the recipient.

Entities Detail. System 2 entities are predominantly *organizations*. The distinctive element of the organizations in System 2 that does not exist in System 1 (economy) is *reliance on involuntary external inflows* from System 1 or other forms of inflows from System 2 (i.e. Sys2 Subsystem 3's fiat money, to be discussed). These organizations are typically in administrative units at different scales (from local to supranational, broadly referred to as *governments,* * or *states*), and have sub-units such as departments, ministries, agencies, elective bodies, etc., each charged with diverse tasks and missions. A distinction should be made between *central* governments (whether national or supranational) and more *local* (state/provincial, county/parish, municipalities, etc.).

*****Note**: The term *government* can be misleading because *any* financial entity, whether in System 1 or 2 has some form of governing body including households, businesses/corporations, and other organizations (Re: corporate governance). At the individual level, *self-governance* exists in the form of decision-making and taking (or not taking) actions for survival and well-being. Also see the section below describing various income sources of entities.

Income Sources. Many governmental entities do not rely on derivative inflows and earn income through voluntary means: Admission fees, rental income (common area fees included or separate), tuitions/course fees, association/membership fees and donations. Partial or fully self-contained examples include amusement parks and some retirement resorts (with their own road systems); Disney World; some university and college campuses; nudist/naturist colonies; some campgrounds; some religious organizations or church-run communities; some cruises (esp. long-term arrangements); contractual communities and homeowner's associations (HOAs); managed mobile home, RV, trailer parks and resorts.

This can also apply to any localities that function as *providers* (of *local area management*): For example, property owners are charged a flat contractual fee with opt-out provisions such that property owners can switch providers if they are dissatisfied with the service (this assumes a competitive market for such providers which may be relatively undeveloped now).

In addition to general administrative functions, financial entities' actors in each of Sys2's subsystems also redistribute funds, and buy and sell votes (the buying and selling of votes can be described as part of the process of *rent-seeking*). The rent-seekers are typically from Sys1 attempting to gain advantages from the *power to override* in Sys2 (also see Sys2 Subsystems 2 and 3), and can include *rent-seeking* by Sys2 entities as well. Rent-seekers also may include the term transfer-seeking and may involve *special interest groups* acting to obtain unearned benefits from System 2 [Re: Public choice theory; also see Olson 1971].

Subsystems of System 2

System 2 Inflows and Subsystems

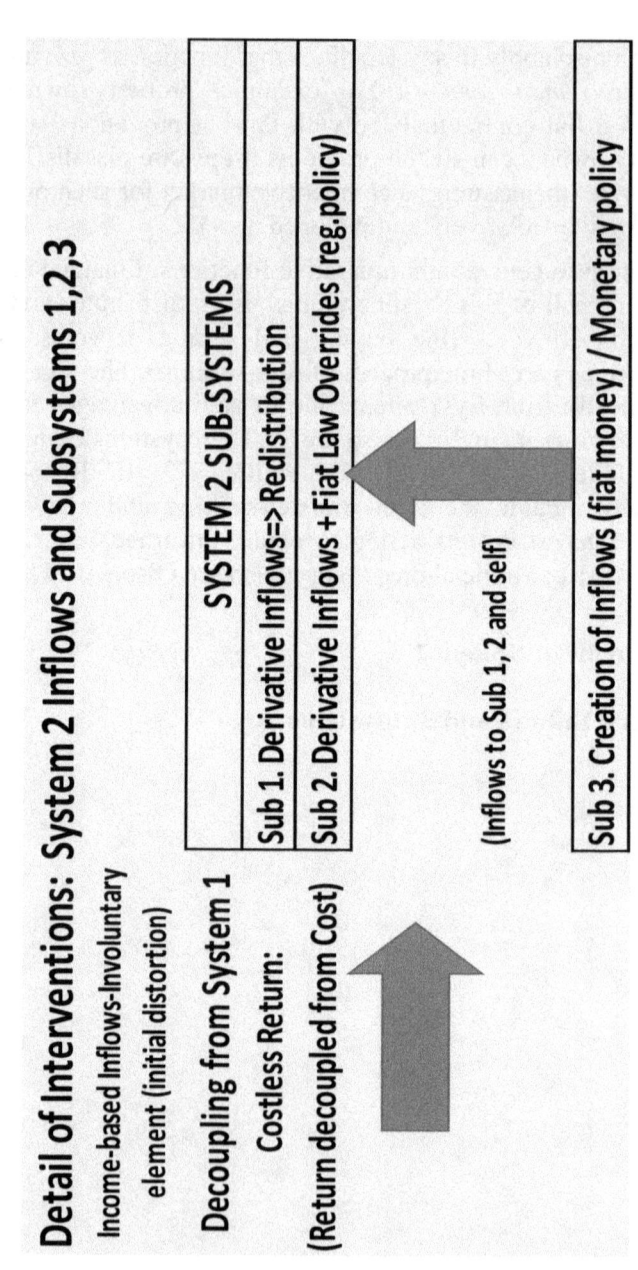

System 2 is assumed to be comprised of three fundamental subsystems that rely upon derivative inflows and share a common aim of maximizing inflows; each subsystem has different functions as detailed further below. Subsystem 3 is unique in its capability to create its *own* inflows with fiat money, and supplement the inflows of the other two subsystems. Subsystems may also be abbreviated as "Sub"; accordingly, Subsystem 2 policy 2 can be written "Sub2.2" or "Sub2. Policy 2."

Polarity and Feedback Loop: System 2

System 2's dominant polarity is *positive*, described by a *reinforcing* feedback loop. The posited feedback loops and delays of System 2's three sub-systems are summarized in the table below, along.

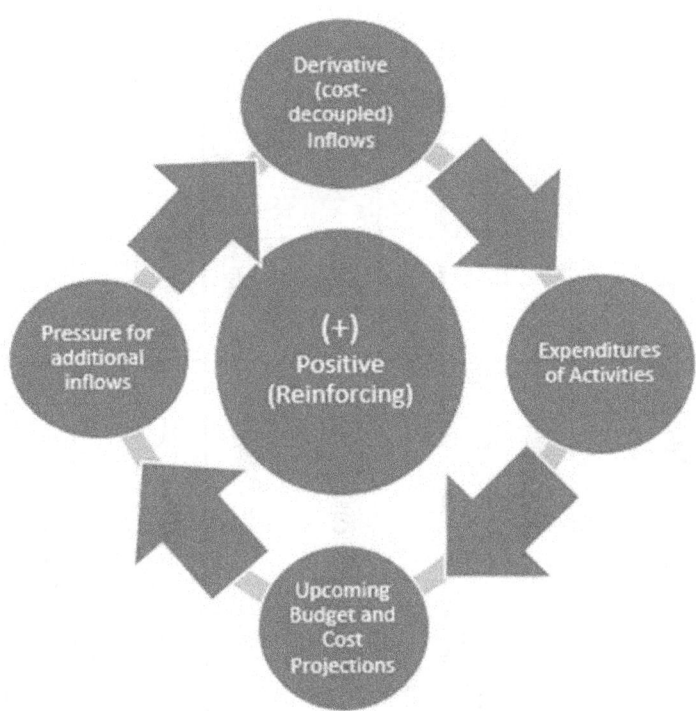

SYSTEM 2 SUB-SYSTEMS FEEDBACK LOOP SUMMARY

1	Inflows => Redistribution	*	*	*			
2	Inflows + Overriding Interventions (reg/policy)	*	*	*	*	*	*
3	Creation of inflows + Overriding Interventions (fiat money)				*	*	*

Feedback Loop Progression	Phase 1 (Ph1) Reinforcing- Non Fiat Money	Ph1 Delay 1 Overshoot- Expenditures> Inflows	Ph1 Delay 2 Reversal	Phase 2 (Ph2) Reinforcing -Fiat Money (national-supranational)	Ph2 Delay 1 Overshoot- debt repayment	Ph.2 Delay 2 Reversal
Subsystem 1 (columns)	F, G, H, I, J	K	L, M, N			
Subsystem 2 (columns)	F, G, H, I, J	K	L, M, N			
Subsystem 3 (columns)				F, G, H, I, J	K	L, M, N

Financing of Subsystem Activities: Detail

Initially it is assumed that there is no *fiat money* to assist in the financing of these redistributive policies. The dominant source of financing is initially (a) taxation (here referred to as *derivative inflows* or *income-based fees*); and (b) bond financing (issuance of government bonds to the public, not purchased with central bank high-powered money).

Other Sources of Financing. However, should these non-fiat money sources dry up, the third major source (c) *high-powered money* (*base money*) may be resorted to as a back-up source. The fiat element of System 2 is the focus of Subsystem 3.

For details on the financing constraints on government activities known as the *government budget restraint* (GBR) or *government budget constraint* (GBC), refer to Christ (1968, 1979).

Other potentially expanding sources of funds considered here are *penalties and fines* (such as for anti-trust violations; Re: European Union Commission; U.S. anti-trust law), and in a recent development, fiat *crypto-currencies*, which have the potential to leverage central bank fiat money by many multiples as discussed in **Sub3.6**.

Subsystem 2 (Sub2) also is financed through a mix of the sources described above and can grant favors to both System 1 and System 2 financial entities through *fiat law* and the power of *overriding authority backed by force*, including *invasive* force.

Many financial entities (e.g. businesses) engage in what is called *rent-seeking* to secure legislation for fiat laws (granting the power to override existing laws) that bring them advantages. In Subsystem 2, aspiring political figures "buy" votes (political support) in exchange for the rent-seekers "selling" their votes; they can do this by promising to use their power to override existing rules and bypass the judicial system even when redress through the courts is possible (Re: *extra-judicial* actions). Rent-seekers can be both Sys1 or Sys2 actors seeking legal privilege.

This nature will become clearer when we look at the details of the policy tables below.

Administration and Interventions: Detail

Interventions generally refer to fiat law and *policy* interventions; these are essentially *enforceable rules* established through the legislative process* and administered by bureaucracies; a separate lawmaking domain called *administrative law* is discussed below.
or depending on the nature of the political structure, by executive or similar order.

A principal source for interventions can vary and include *rent-seeking* by intended beneficiaries of the policy (See **Col F** for likely instances of rent-seeking, and **Col D** for likely beneficiaries of wealth transfer). The rent-seekers may also work closely with candidates for political office, and back-room deals between them may also result in considerable wealth transfer to those political figures (whether incumbent or if elected) in addition to the rent-seekers. (This is noted in **Col D** as "via political support.")
In some cases, policies that tend to serve special interests are also supported by groups that advocate for them based on moral intentions including fairness and safety, although the contradiction is not always apparent. Also, in some cases convincing policy recommendations can originate from individuals or organizations deemed to be authorities on the subject; this relates to the critical topics of *naïve interventionism* (where harm is caused with the innocent intent to help), *iatrogenics* as applied to the social sciences (e.g. where economists advise on policy), and the *expert problem* (Taleb 2012: 114-118, 215).

Bureaucracy. The build-up of bureaucracies is also expected to be a natural outgrowth of the positive reinforcing feedback loop of System 2 within various administrative units. Both a combination of reliance on derivative inflows and *legal purchasing requirements* (see Subsystem 2 detail) for users rather than voluntary buyer demand exist, leading to a higher likelihood of longer waiting lines and staffing shortages at offices involving customer service (unless intentionally managed otherwise). The shortages described here are not of the same nature as in Col H. of the subsystems. Here, the reinforcing feedback loop of System 2 requires that *more derivative inflows* be supplied (e.g. larger budgets) to incent the bureaucracy to increase staffing to serve customer needs. A general outcome is a hypothesized lower increase in productivity relative to private enterprise (On bureaucracy, Mises (1944); Re: *Baumol's disease*, or *Baumol's Growth Disease* (Nordhaus 2006).

Recall the financing sources for the subsystems noted above. Importantly, the *mix of financing inflows* is expected to impact the level of customer service; for example, in a bureaucratic office of System 2, if customers themselves are a dominant and direct source of the inflows (such as for *user fees, licenses, permits*) it is possible that the administrative unit will be somewhat more responsive to customers; nevertheless it is still likely that the unit's inflows are a combination of *both* their annual *budgets* (coming from derivative inflows from a central administrative unit) plus *direct customer fees*.

Administrative Law. A significant form of regulation and policy, *administrative law* (Berman 1983) originates from a different source and may display a somewhat different dynamic than that of rent-seeking and vote-buying as seen in the electoral system. Nevertheless, businesses may attempt rent-seeking with bureaucrats-- the more bureaucratic control in the system, the more likely bureaucratic favor will be sought in exchange for certain favors, including post-retirement positions in the private sector). Administrative law originates from the bureaucracies that are charged with implementation of laws; many aspects of laws and regulations are not entirely spelled out when written and may require interpretation by the staff of the applicable agencies in charge. This body of law is assumed to emerge somewhat independently from the others with its own reinforcing feedback loop leading to *bureaucratic overreach* and possibly with similar impacts as the feedback loop of the rent-seeking elements of Subsystem 2.

Phases of Dominant Feedback Loops

Initial Phase: Reinforcing. System 2's dominant polarity is *positive*, described by a *reinforcing* feedback loop, driven by Subsystem 1 and 3; Subsystem 2's rent-seeking and interventions/overrides may contribute to an acceleration of the process as income falters. In a reinforcing feedback loop, rising inflows for a System 2 financial entity leads to increased *use* of those inflows (called *expenditures*) and pressure for further increases in inflows (i.e. annual requests for budget increases), resulting in a high probability of *excessive charges* (of income-based fees) onto System 1's actors. As previously noted, the involuntary nature of these charges begins the *decoupling* process (decoupling of cost from return), and gives rise to two feedback loops, one in System 1 which is *counterbalancing* and aims to reduce this perceived excessive cost, and the dominant feedback loop of System 2 described by the reinforcing pattern of rising expenditures (=inflows) that tend to be followed by more pressure for rising expenditures (=inflows). Costs do not exist in the same sense as in System 1, and therefore in Sys2 the term "cost" is likely to be used as a *decline in inflows*.

The long-term impact of both feedback loops working in opposition is likely to be increased deficits and debt accumulation in System 2, followed by the delayed phase of overshoot-reversal.

Subsequent Phases: Overshoot-Reversal. Actual cost reductions will occur in a reversal phase, but generally not until an "overshoot" point has been reached, exemplified by a *fiscal crisis* of some sort. The crisis is characterized by outlays exceeding tax receipts, likely accompanied by an accumulating payables backlog. The administrative unit will focus on preserving what it considers to be its core priority payments such as employee payrolls, retirement pensions and interest on the debt. Unpaid bills may result in lawsuits and collections efforts by various parties including subcontractors and recipients of other benefits.

Reversal. The general designation of the post-overshoot phase is reversal, which for example, consists of several scenarios detailed in Column L, but where crackdowns, budget cuts and cost controls, as well as deregulation/liberalization may tend to be predominant. An S-Curve is also a possible outcome in which a plateau is temporarily reached. In extreme cases, the overshoot could be followed by an eventual *collapse* which, depending on the scale could take various forms including a regime change or in the case of a hyperinflation/currency collapse, a currency re-issue.
:
Subsystem 2. As with Subsystem 1 and 3, Subsystem 2 also has an initial *reinforcing* feedback loop but of a different nature. Rent-seeking can be rewarded with fiat law overrides that may act as a catalyst that *accelerates* a decline in income flows in the long-term, leading to a possibly faster "overshoot" of debt accumulation and fiscal crisis as described for Subsystems 1 and 2. As with Subsystems 1 and 3, in a delayed manner, a reversal may occur in which prior overrides (regulations) will be replaced with deregulation, liberalization, and other means to raise inflows **(Col L).**

Subsystem 3 is posited to be a *financing* extension of Subsystem 1 when more inflows are needed than are available from income-based (tax) inflows alone (occurring in the "overshoot" phase with deficits and debt accumulation). Subsystem 3's mechanics usually apply to national level (central or national governments, also called nation-states) because these typically rely on central bank financing through the capability of fiat money creation. Supranational central banks are also in existence (e.g. European Central Bank ECB) as part of the E.U.'s *monetary union*; although there is no *fiscal union*, it may be possible for national bonds to be purchased by the ECB to help finance national expenditures and redistribution aims of Subsystem 1.

After resources in the first *non-fiat money* phase have been exhausted, central bank-endowed states can avail themselves of fiat money and cheap borrowing to continue inflows and the reinforcing dynamic progresses. Here too, in a delayed phase (Phase 2 Delay 2), Subsystem 3 eventually is expected to experience an overshoot where debt repayment capability becomes insufficient, and then a subsequent reversal or even some form of "collapse" in some cases. The term "collapse" is often used for dramatic effect, but for a nation-state with a central bank, a likely scenario would be a collapse of the currency's value, and reissue of a "new" currency. In more extreme cases, the governing body (e.g. the nation-state) may also face an abrupt regime change.

Forecasted Timeframe of Loops. Due to complexity, it is considered impossible to forecast the longevity of a feedback loop of policies and outcomes from start to end. However, from a historical standpoint one example corresponding to the dominant interventions in **Sub2.2** is about 73 years: The former Soviet Union (1918-1991); although it should be clarified that without the tacit permission and existence of underground private markets/trading activity (black markets), collapse might have come much earlier.

In the monetary realm of Subsystem 3, the policy origins and other factors involved in asset bubble-crash cycles can vary considerably. For stock markets, 8-10 years might be a rough guess, but subject to change with policy and technological changes, as well.

Acceleration of Feedback Loops and Self-Destructive Policies. It should be noted that implementation of certain policies is expected to act as catalysts that *accelerate* some feedback loops: System 2's own inflow-maximization goal can also be adversely affected by these policy actions. Unaware of the feedback loop impacts, policymakers and officials may implement policies with *self-destructive outcomes* that either impoverish the cost-bearers (**Col E**), cause *disincentives* to produce or earn income, or simply destroy wealth (Re: Deadweight cost of taxes).

In a later phase of a *reinforcing feedback loop* officials may attempt to reverse the negative impacts by removing certain policies (See **Col L**). Also critical is *moral hazard* at the policy level: **Sub3.3b** for the impact of fiat money in cushioning the impacts of policies that contribute to poverty (income reduction).

Sub1.1a (price controls), **Sub2.2a** central planning (expropriations, etc.) and **Sub2.2b** (private property bans) are also notable examples.

Use of Force in System 2
When there are problems involving safety of person or property and other means are not possible, a critical question is what kind of force is appropriate. In System 2, at the point of involuntary derivative inflows based on income of System 1 actors, there is an invasive element. Apart from this, it is assumed that while the dominant form of force remains *defensive* force, keeping out or repelling intruders as in System 1. However, there is assumed to be a greater likelihood of *invasive* force (e.g. forced entry onto private property or physically restraining someone), justified with the *original decoupling* (involuntary purchases due to perceived excessive fees as described above). Invasive force is likely to be used relating to perceived threats to the system's own security such as in *protests and social unrest*, as well as secondary policy responses in the form of *crackdowns* (**Col L**). These crackdowns are typically the result of *delayed* impacts of System 2's own prior *interventions* into System 1.

Wealth Accumulation in System 2
To the extent that the inflows into System 2 from System 1 are derived from System 1, there is a *transfer of wealth* for which no return is received by those who bear the cost, *other than* (a) for the voluntary portion of inflows that represent *commensurate* services provided (recall from above that this is an amount that is paid in exchange for services provided that would have been paid anyway and is therefore perceived to be *voluntary*; (b) through rent-seeking in which some redistributed funds may be directed to the rent-seeker through political support for a candidate who then delivers the special privileges.

Note that a Sys1 entity that receives redistributed benefits (such as *transfer payments, contracts, direct employment, special compensation)* from System 2 and saves part of it to invest is not necessarily adding to overall wealth as the inflows from System 1 have already been earned and have simply been redistributed.

Punitive fines could be treated as a form of retribution for damages caused, although the extent of the damages might ultimately need to be determined through the judicial system involving long court battles.

The mechanics of transfer of wealth differs for fiat money as is it not a straight redistribution of inflows but involves the creation of new inflows, to be detailed in the Subsystem 3 table and discussion.

Emergence of Economic Distortions

Origins. Economic distortions are posited to stem primarily from policy interventions or forceful actions that give rise to the following: Cost-Return decoupling and disproportionality (interrelated). A third origin which may not necessarily be policy-based is *perception management*, discussed further below.

(1) **Cost-Return Decoupling**: Decoupling of the cost and associated return such that the cost is borne by one party and transferred to another party as their (costless) return. This occurs *without the express consent* of the party that bears the cost. Simply and broadly stated, *someone involuntarily bears the cost while* someone *else (or no-one else) * receives the net benefit associated with that cost.*

*****Note**: No-one else: See the discussion regarding *dead-weight cost of taxes* below.

The *decoupling* is seen both in the *fundamental* decoupling linking System 1 and System 2, as well as the cost-return decoupling in the policy tables: The actors in **Col D** are largely the beneficiaries of unjust wealth while the costs are borne by those in **Col E**.

Interrelated with *cost-return decoupling* is:

(2) **Cost-Return Disproportionality**. Where the proportion of the benefit (return) received exceeds the proportion of the cost borne --cost-bearing is lesser than return in some proportion (or zero).

This necessarily includes the concept of *cost avoidance*, where all or part of the *cost of one's actions* is avoided; for example, this cost includes an offender facing no sanctions/punishment for causing damages to others, or to the environment, etc.). See **Sub2.3d Sub2.5b, Sub2.5c)** for examples of cost transference, cost avoidance, *judicial immunity*, and avoidance of accountability.

(3) **Perception Management** (discussed after the following section)

Embodiment of Distortions
Distortions become embodied within economic activity in at least two important ways:
(1) Through *incentives* on human (and business) behavior, such as incentives/disincentives to produce or earn more income in a broader sense, incentives, or disincentives to take some action *or not to act*) (Becker 1976; Schultz 1978 Re: distortions of incentives in agriculture/food production).
The combination of incentives to (a) *reduce income* (to lower costs associated with generating income such as income-based fees/taxes; regulatory burdens, etc.) and to (b) *increase one's own cost-decoupled returns* by becoming dependent on transfer payments supplied by System 2 is an example of how incentives underlie the reinforcing feedback loop of System 2.
(2) These distorted human and business incentives may tend to be reflected in *price*s and the *pricing system* (*prices as signals*); related to pricing are distortions in *costs* and *income* (Note that a cost-bearing by one person can be part of the income of another). (Hayek 1931, 1945, 1974; on production/overproduction (gluts) and pricing: Say 1803, Sowell 1973; Hutt 1974; Manhattan Institute 1983).

(3) **Perception Management**. A less obvious but nevertheless a possibly significant source of distortions of human behavior may be *perception management* by various groups including the mass

media, public officials, businesses, or religious and other organizations. The distortive impacts may be much more significant where *centralization* and *centrally-planned* systems (see **Sub2.2**) are concerned, and/or when an entity has a monopoly on the control and dissemination of information. An insidious form of perception management might be thought to include the spreading of *rumors* (either false or embellished based on some kernel of evidence) as well as efforts to silence certain individuals or organizations by means of *ritual defamation* or *character assassination* (Also Re: disinformation).

Sub2.1c details System 2 *official* attempts at perception management and *disinformation*. It should be clarified that the attempt at disinformation is not limited to System 2.

In System 1 it is entirely possible for groups and individuals to spread rumors, innuendo and lies about others to discredit them; however, a major difference is the relatively larger concentration of power and centralization of information that traditionally has resided in System 2 entities. Media organizations (newspapers, news outlets and channels, etc.) also might play a role in disseminating official (dis)information under the guise of factuality (Re: fake news)

Prices as Signals. Prices convey signals that should reflect with some degree of accuracy (although assumed to always be imperfect) information about changes in our environment and how best to respond to those changes.

An extreme case of price distortion would be when in response to a *supply shock* (with demand unchanged) and/or a sudden increase in demand, prices would be expected to rise, but due to a policy-originated distortion, prices are *falling* instead. This sends a signal that there is less of a need than there in fact is, increasing the likelihood of *shortages* (See **Col H**).

Another extreme case involves the absence or near absence of a pricing system altogether, characteristic of centrally-planned economies; leading to eventual breakdown of economic processes (Mises 1920; Voslensky 1984; Smirnov 2015; also see **Sub2.2**).

Col G through **Col J** indicate where price distortions are likely to exist, leading to the outcomes shown. Notable examples specifically targeting prices are price controls (**Sub2.1a**), controls on *interest rates* (price of borrowing funds; **Sub 3.1**) and on *wages* (price of labor; see **Sub2.4a, Sub2.4b**).

A commonly overlooked example of distorted prices are public sector contract bids as detailed in **Sub1.2**; the reason for this is that the costs were borne by the income-based payers (taxpayers), and sent as derivative inflows to System 2 for public contracts; these funds are typically controlled and administered by public officials, bureaucrats or politicians and through a bidding process or by private deal-making* and then granted to contractors The result can be *inflated bids*, *padding* and *overbilling*. This can be widespread when heavy infrastructure, public works and public housing projects are involved in economic development, or social policy, as discussed in further detail in **Col D**.

*There is a strong incentive to arrange special deals with those who control the funds to secure contracts; see the discussion on *corruption* and *bribes*, elsewhere.

Distortion-Embodied Prices and Costs. While it is generally recognized that prices contain valuable information and act as crucial signals for economic activity (Hayek 1945; Bowles, et al. 2017), the crucial role of *distortions embodied in prices themselves* may be given less attention or poorly understood. These distortions as reflected in price (prices as signals) can give rise to second-order incentives (or disincentives) that can lead to instability and crises.

A thorough analysis of price distortions must examine the *source* of the economic distortions that are embodied in the prices. It is recognized that distortive impacts on prices and interactions can be exceedingly complex; *non-linearities* are expected to be the norm. Quantification and identification of embodied distortions is by no means an easy task. However, it is hoped that this model together with economic and *price theory* can offer a useful framework for capturing the dominant forces (Re" Price Theory; Friedman 1986; Stigler 1987). In combination with *complexity theory* (Fellman, et al 2016, Bar-Yam 2005, Sayama 2015), and *system dynamics* (Forrester, 1971), understanding can be further improved upon.

Cost-Return Decoupling and Disproportionality: Other Points

Deadweight Costs. It should be noted that in some cases, it is possible that someone (e.g. producers and consumers) can be forced to bear the cost of an intervention while *no-one else* receives the return due to the *wealth destruction* occurring from the intervention itself; a case in point concerns income-based taxation (e.g. taxation on goods and/or services such as sales, consumption, or value-added taxes; Re: *Deadweight cost of taxes*).

*Recall from above that the cost borne is considered involuntary when the income-based payer perceives that the costs for services being provided are at some point excessive.

Immutability (Lack of "Opt-Out") Moreover, the decoupling intervention may tend to be "locked in" by the regulatory apparatus and policies of System 2. In other words, other than by legislative means, there is usually no *"opt out"* provision. * Moreover, many jurisdictions are legal monopolies and are not subject to competition from alternative providers (e.g. municipalities).

*In response, and integral to the reinforcing feedback loop, *outmigration (moving to another jurisdiction) or reducing income adversely impact on the jurisdiction's finances.*

Policy interventions are not typically subject to adjustment, except for by a *political process* that may be time-consuming and exceedingly difficult to achieve even if successful, as many parties will likely be competing for the inflows or benefits. Protests may erupt against changes in previous benefits discouraging further downward adjustments in expenditures.

In pricing policy, the interventions or bureaucratic edicts controlling/establishing the *pricing* of goods are not easily and swiftly adjustable to rapidly changing market conditions, consumer demand and cost dynamics; the economic distortions from such a policy intervention can give rise to serious financial and economic problems, some with catastrophic consequences, as will be described below.

Comparison of Systemic Distortions

Economic distortions are generally defined as impacting upon System 1, *economy*. The term *systemic* is simplistically defined as a set of rules and procedures.

System 2-Originated. A System 2 intervention into System 1 can result in an economic distortion in System 1 that is called *System2-originated*. This is the subject of the policy intervention classifications of System 2 and its Subsystems 1, 2 and 3.

System 1-Originated. Systemic economic distortions also are assumed to originate within System 1 that do not have a System 2 origin and are not based in any policy interventions. These can be called *System 1-originated* distortions.

Because of constant change in our environment, *all* price changes could be in theory described as embodying some (basic) level of (natural) distortions at least in terms of erroneous information. Here the key distinction must be made: Distortions are assumed to exist when the reality of costs (and returns) is not (approximately) accurately reflected in the price. If prices are changing *approximately* in tandem with changes in the underlying costs and returns, then the prices could be assumed to be *approximately* undistorted (approximately because of the assumed lack of perfect information). The above definition might be clarified with a few examples.

Natural Disaster Example: Supply Shocks. If a massive heat wave, storm or cold snap suddenly reduces supplies of essentials, information about the reduced supply relative to the demand (if demand remains roughly the same as before) is typically reflected in rising prices of those crops--these prices serve as signals that embody information about the level of damage (reduced supply) caused by the weather abnormality. The higher price may tend to attract potential sellers (from outside of the affected areas) to supply the market until consumers needs are satisfied and the price stabilizes (downward).

Conservation Link. Although often overlooked, a higher price also serves as a signal to *conserve* on use of the resource.

Presence and Absence of Distortions. As a starting point, if information about reduced supplies and demand is reflected such that the *direction* of the price signal is roughly correct (less supply, same or higher demand, higher price) then a price distortion may be less likely. If for some reason the prices remain unchanged or are *falling* while demand is the same or rising while supply has dried up, then a distortion would be suspected and the risk of shortages rises. A crucial question at that juncture would be the source of such a distortion of information about the demand-supply reality. Price-gouging laws are well-meaning attempts to prevent exploitation of natural disaster victims, but their interference with pricing could lead to a second round of victims when price distortions discourage delivery of badly needed supplies (Re: price-gouging; Perry, 2017). Keeping prices of badly-needed supplies artificially low also encourages overuse and more rapid diminution of supplies. Often overlooked are *location/accessibility* and *quantities* of goods sold as factors of pricing: For example, physically transporting supplies to remote areas in inclement weather and dangerous conditions without power; the sale of a *single* item at a very high mark-up vs. the per-unit cost of a case or palette of the same item.

Persistent vs. Temporary. The question also arises whether price distortions tend to *persist*, or whether they are self-correcting after a *temporary error* due to bad information. *Perception management* (**Sub2.1c**) may play a role in both systems; how quickly the pricing distortions are corrected may depend in part on the level of control and *centralization* of information, as well as the *belief systems* of customers. A System 2 distortion may tend to remain in place indefinitely as long as the policy can continue to be strictly enforced, or until there is disruption (e.g. shortages) that induces a policy change. The control of information in System 2 is noted in **Sub2.1c**.

Asset Market Example. First, a distortion in the context of *asset prices* should be explained: Prices becoming unhinged from some theoretical measure of *fundamentals*. Fundamentals can be defined in various ways; for equities, a common fundamental is a return measure such as net *income*.

Investors/speculators purchase assets in the hopes of realizing *capital gains* or perhaps as long-term holdings. Even without any System 2 policy interventions (or *anticipated* policy changes), it is entirely possible that the prices of assets can become distorted and bid up to unsustainable levels after which their prices collapse. Possible *triggers* for such a System 1-originated distortion include:

1. Forward-looking factors involving new technological developments and discoveries;

2. The concept of *"castles in the air"* (Malkiel 2006)

3. Notably strong recent performance of the firm, beating earnings estimates, etc.

4. Emotional factors, optimism, and enthusiasm;

5. Cultural or philosophical trends and changes.

6. Manipulation by promoters via false rumors and *pump-and-dump*, among other dishonest tactics.

Conversely, sudden asset price collapses and associated capital losses can occur due to a variety of factors originating within System 1 such as unexpected poor performance of a company, sudden management shakeup, lawsuits, technological change, competitive environment, etc.

Key Distinction between Systems. It should be emphasized that System 1-originated distortions, while they are expected to occur, are generally considered to be less pronounced and subject to greater counterbalancing forces than System 2-originated distortions. Returning to asset markets, System 2 is believed to primarily have positive (reinforcing) feedback loops that can push prices/values to greater extremes than would be likely without System 2 interventions.

PART II. SUBSYSTEM AND POLICY TABLES

Part II is divided according to the policy tables for each subsystem of System 2: Subsystem 1, 2 and 3. Beginning horizontally, the first section just below covers the columns A through N. Next, each of the three subsystems is presented with discussion of their specific policy interventions.

Abbreviations for the Policy Tables. Examples: **Sub1.4a** means Subsystem 1, policy 4a; **Sub2.4a Col B** refers to column B of Subsystem 1 policy 4a. The subsystem and policy tables are also abbreviated *policy tables*.

Column Categories: Feedback Loop Progression

A. Policy Intervention Type
B. Level/Scale
C. Rhetorical Justification
D. Decoupling: Returns portion. Wealth gains (via the offering of political and financial support); income/Wealth distorted upwards.
E. Decoupling: Costs portion. Cost-Bearers: bearing the cost (et incomes/wealth reduced).

Phase 1 (Initial)

F. Rent-Seeking Activity
G. Impaired Production/Reduced Income Impacts
H. Shortages (including food crises)
I. Black Markets and violence due to contract non-legality
J. Clustering: Oversupply/Excessive Speculation and Competition

Delay 1-Overshoot

K. Deficit/Debt (Expenditures>Inflows)

Delay 2-Reversal (also possible S-Curve or Collapse)

L. Secondary Policies/Impacts (including state violence)
M. Ownership Insecurity (including self-ownership); hoarding
N. Visible Protests/Unrest

Feedback Loop Progression and Phases. The column order from left to right starting from F is only an approximate progression and may vary according to the subsystem and a variety of factors; non-linear effects must be taken to account, as well. The number "1" indicates an assumed *elevated risk* of an occurrence, not a probability of 1 or 100%.; the probabilities are not known, but considered high enough to note as a risk. Comments may also appear in the boxes for further explanation. *Blank* boxes have an ambiguity in that the risk of occurrence is either not known, unclear, or less likely.

Each column is briefly explained below.

Column A. Policy Intervention Type: These are the interventions that are imposed or implemented within System 2 that may impact on both System 1 and System 2. Policy interventions are assumed to originate from actors within both Sys1 and Sys2, two principal ones being (a) *rent-seeking businesses* (Sys1) selling their votes and support to gain special advantages from the override authority of Sys2, and (b) vote-buying officials seeking election in Sys2. Once law, the intervention is imposed upon the relevant areas of System 1.

Column B. Level/Scale: These are the typical administrative units within System 2 from "local" (townships, municipalities/municipal corporations, and counties/parishes, then to more "regional" such as states, prefectures, and provinces. The national level is typically the largest unit, *although supranational entities* exist; even without *fiscal union*, a supranational entity may still have a Subsystem 2 with certain regulatory bodies and the powers to *fine* and a Subsystem 3 (fiat money/monetary policy (Re: European Union; European Central Bank).

Column C. Rhetorical Justification: These are "rhetorical" because they are the words/concepts used to justify the intervention that many would either agree with or feel generally unopposed to. Major categories are: Growth, Stability, Security,

Fairness/Morality. "Jobs" may also be included in the growth category. More than one of the terms might be coupled together for additional persuasion.

There can be a significant confusion between intentions/rhetoric and actual outcomes. The stated goals may generally be laudable, and can gain broad public support, playing on the emotions of the public, but the outcomes can result in the *opposite* of what is intended.

Refer to the policy tables, which indicate where unjust wealth gains are justified rhetorically (**Col D**), as well as those who bear the cost (the cost-bearers) of the policies (**Col E**).

Each justification should be examined individually.

It is critical to note that the judiciary can be called upon to redress wrongs, but the judicial system may be *bypassed* by the overriding authority of fiat law of the subsystems. Important concerns regarding the judicial system are also addressed in **Sub2.3d** and **Sub2.5d** (also **Sub2.5c**).

The rhetorical justifications are enumerated and explained below in the following order: 1. security/protection; 2. growth/stability; and 3. fairness/morality. This third rhetorical justification is particularly important as a force for policy actions and deserves special attention because those policies are superficially very appealing but can have wide-ranging adverse impacts upon economies. In extreme cases, policies to ostensibly promote fairness or morality have played significant roles in catastrophic outcomes, including famine (Lofchie 1978; Schultz 1978), relocations and genocide (**Sub2.4d**). Also refer to the Appendix Ideology, Morality and Political Systems grounded in forms of fairness policy.

1. Security/Protection. Security and protection are also praiseworthy objectives and are to be taken very seriously; this encompasses societal order including the protection of property and respect of voluntary contracts. Policies to improve security are generally popular and may often be combined with *nationalism* (it should be added that nationalism does not necessarily imply support for a specific political party or system and therefore political figures of various parties and ideologies are expected to appeal to nationalism/love of country for support).

Although every case varies, security is invoked to protect the people from supposed dangerous group(s), entities, foreign products, or a variety of potential threats to livelihood or the environment.

The question is about outcomes: The importance of the goal of security is understood, but will security in fact be achieved by implementation of the proposed policies; should the policies fail, it is also not clear whether responsibility will be properly assigned to the proponents of the policies (Re: accountability, skin in the game).

Labelling of "enemies" may also be a feature and can be based on race/ethnicity, national origin, religion, the wealthy and powerful, etc. In extreme cases, for purposes of "public safety", certain groups are targeted for removal or denial of entry, however defined. A major concern and potential danger is if the judicial system is bypassed (or if a system of impartial justice) during the implementation phase of a security-related policy, many innocents may be targeted (See **Sub2.3d**, **Sub2.5d** and **Sub2.5c**).

Such proposals may also be linked to requests for funding for various security/safety-related expenditures (purchases, contracts), construction projects.

For mercantilist reasons, blocking foreign products from market entry may be proposed due to their supposed public health safety concerns. Examples also include: Policies supporting subsidization of certain industries or price supports, etc. for security purposes, whether for national security, or food security.

Moreover, one component of security is "stability" of the economy as it can be argued that unstable economic conditions can pose a threat to security. (Also see growth/stability).

2. Growth/Stability (including *jobs/employment*). Policy proposals are generally a positive message to grow or "stimulate" the economy and bring back jobs. Phrases like "rebuilding our crumbling infrastructure" may also elicit popular approval and be popular with *special interest groups* such as contractors. For some countries, an important policy goal has been *autarky* or "national self-sufficiency" often accompanied by heavy industrial policy and controls on trade to maintain national dominance and to restrict foreign imports unless used for technological superiority.
In some extreme historical cases, growth policies are associated with "development dictatorships" which may ignore or grant immunity to offenders later to be found responsible for environmental and/or health damage. (Re: Morinaga Milk poisoning case, Minamata Disease). By treating these businesses with impunity, *the costs of their actions* are artificially (by policy) lowered. (See **Sub2.5b** and **Sub2.5c**)

Jobs/Employment. A component of the growth agenda is increasing jobs and/or prospects for employment. A common misconception is that job growth and prospects are *independent of* the business and economic environment. Put another way, since labor involves a cost, businesses can be expected to have certain pre-conditions for additional hiring; anything that unfairly or unnecessarily increases costs of businesses can create disincentives to further add *labor* as a cost. Defining unnecessary/necessary or unfair/fair costs is subjective, but is in part addressed in the policy discussions and detailed particularly in **Col D** and **Col E**.

As noted above, *stability* can also be linked to the popular policy of national security, as it can be argued that unstable economic conditions can pose a threat to security.

3. Fairness and Morality

Morality--what is moral and right—is a powerful force for political action, and can bolster popularity for many policies that propose to deliver fairness. The importance of this element of the system dynamics cannot be underestimated. The appeal to morality can be through the rhetoric of fairness, or through the moral high ground of religious and other ideologies. Note that even *non*-religious ideologies can have qualities akin to religions, and can form the basis of calls for policy change for moral reasons.

Three critical points must be made:

Goals and Outcomes: Distinction. Critical to understand and as is noted elsewhere, *outcomes* of policies, once implemented, may differ considerably from the stated *goals*, such as *fairness* or to *advance the cause of social justice*. Most would agree that goal of fairness is moral and praiseworthy, but often misunderstood is that proposed policies to correct for injustices may not achieve their desired outcome(s); worse, and tragically, there is considerable evidence that the *opposite* of what is intended can also occur, to the point of famine and genocide (See the policies and history under the heading of **Sub2.2, Sub2.4d, Sub2.5c**)

Ulterior Motives and Unintended Consequences?
It is essential to identify whether policies promoting fairness and/or appealing to morality are in fact intended to serve particular interests. Unbeknownst to many proponents and supporters is that policies proposed to advance fairness and moral purposes can serve to transfer wealth *unjustly* to favored groups through *rent-seeking* and the *vote-buying* process, as noted elsewhere. Some

contradictions and blind spots are detailed in the next section below.

Rhetoric and Reality: Contradictions of Fairness Policies

The policy tables indicate where unjust wealth gains are justified rhetorically by fairness/justice (**Col D**), as well as those who bear the cost (the cost-bearers) of the policies **(Col E)**. Also refer to the historical record: Examples of possible property grabs/transfers through relocation are noted in **Sub2.4d** and in the Appendix under Ideology, Morality, and Political Systems.

Taxpayer Non-Recognition: Ownership of Funds. It should also be noted that in the System 2 arrangement, income-based payers (taxpayers) claims on ownership are not recognized as these funds are both revenues to those firms as well as a form of capital infusion by taxpayers (investment: debt or equity capital). This is noted in **Sub1.2a**, *non-recognition*.

Fairness Policy Supportive of Rent-Seeking (Col F) Although counterintuitive, remarkably, some policies dubbed as "leveling the playing field" or aiming to achieve social justice can result in *crony capitalists* using System 2 machinery using rent-seeking to gain unjust wealth through System 2. See Appendix 2 for further detail on *crony capitalism* among other "isms."

One example of the interwoven nature of crony capitalism and fairness policy relates to Subsystem 3 (fiat money): Those who advocate for much greater redistributive spending create the conditions that would likely benefit crony capitalists such as fiat money-reliant asset managers and hedge funds. How is this possible? Because greater *deficit spending* (government expenditures exceeding revenues) can mean *bond-buying* by central banks to cover the deficit. This pumps new money into the financial system that the investment community can employ to buy up assets and inflate asset prices.

Another example concerns redistributive fairness policies of Subsystem 1: Transfer payments and welfare, housing assistance to the needy are generally supported as advancing the cause of fairness, but the flow of redistributed money is revealing: The funds pass from income-based payers (taxpayers) to government agency administrators, then to the recipients and then to the firms that provide the food, drinks* and other goods they purchase with low-income assistance cards (such as the SNAP program in the U.S.), or real estate developers or lessors in the case of housing allowances and subsidies.

*Note: It should be added that some of the food and drink that qualify for purchases may lack in nutritional value resulting in a possible taxpayer-funded benefit for the so-called "junk food" industry. (USDA, 2016)

Secondary Policies (Col L). Rather than addressing the specific instances of injustice case-by-case or the prior political or judicial origins of privilege and discrimination, *new* policies may be imposed on top of the old ones, causing *new* injustices leading to tensions and internal strife.

Fairness-based policies, although possibly well-intentioned, may entirely bypass solutions that could alleviate economic crises. A case in point from 1966 involved the importation of high-yielding seeds and other technologies from abroad that could have improved agricultural output and alleviated hunger. *Amid a food crisis*, officials and bureaucrats opposed the introduction of new technologies based on social and distributive equity (fairness). Others argued that the seeds exemplified Western cultural hegemony over the country, leading the economy inevitably towards an immoral capitalistic system. (Hopper 1978; also see Shuh (1978) regarding *equity-motivated policies*).

Subsystem 2 Feedback Loop: Production of Fiat Law. What the above examples show, as well as the ability to right wrongs through the *courts*, fairness policy tends to be implemented through *legislation* and *fiat law* which can be quite complex and opaque – beneficiaries may not be fully known and the injustices may not necessarily be corrected by new policies.

This is explained by the emphasis on the ascension to power rather than on the *removal* of power or use of existing tools such as the judiciary to address injustices.

In sum, Subsystem 2 can be described by a reinforcing feedback loop of *fiat law overproduction* in which fiat laws and policies tend to generate more of the same until their economic impacts eventually lead to an overshoot and reversal, or in extreme cases, collapse.

Labels. An important element of the moral force for policy change in favor of fairness lies in the labelling of groups. A case in point is "the wealthy/the rich." The label implies that *all* those who have acquired wealth are suspected dishonesty, whether true or not; in some societies, the desire for fairness also involves targeting a minority (or majority) group deemed to have acquired wealth unjustly and from privilege due to their race and/or ethnicity (Re: National Socialism; Nazism; also see Appendix 2). While unjust wealth and inequality should be addressed, proposals for solving the problem rarely appear to identify a possible connection between existing policy interventions and unjust wealth gains. Regarding wealth inequality and measurement, see Cirillo, et al 2017); Re: Gini coefficient and wealth distribution).

Column D. Decoupling: Returns Portion. Wealth Gains (via the offering of political and financial support).

A decoupling policy intervention that assigns the *return* (*net benefit*) to a particular group (while another group, the cost-bearers, bears the associated cost) is noted here in **Column D**. The beneficiaries may tend to enjoy higher incomes and or wealth through systemic distortions originating from policies.

The group/individuals that bear the cost are shown in **Column E. Political Support in Exchange for Gains**. Col D is also related to **Col F** through *rent-seeking activity*. Rent-seekers hope to gain wealth by offering political support (vote-selling) for those vying for power; in turn, aspiring lawmakers/politicians/officials promise to deliver the benefits (vote-buying). The vote-sellers also may discretely offer *financial* support and payments prior to the ascension to power of the officials, and perhaps also to offer "rewards" (i.e. a share of the wealth gain) while the policy remains in force. Therefore, the wealth gain can be mutual: Both the beneficiary of the policy (businesses and other organizations) as well as the provider of the fiat laws (politicians, lawmakers, officials, etc.). A notable example is the granting of government contracts to private firms through *rigged bidding* (see detail below and in **Sub1.2a, Col D** and **Col H**).

Policy-Aided Cost Avoidance. Note that the wealth gain can also involve policies that help *lower the costs* of one's actions, such as a polluting or dishonest business that seeks to avoid paying the full costs of its actions in some way. For details on cost avoidance, see **Sub2.3b, Sub2.3d, Sub2.4a, Sub2.4d, Sub2.5b, Sub2.5c**.

Political Systems. This political process for support may not be exclusively a phenomenon of *democratic politics*, it is also expected to occur in non-democratic/authoritarian environments, provided that derivative inflows can be secured.

Wealth Gain in a Non-Market Context. In societies that rely heavily on redistribution and non-market pricing to provide certain services, as well as heavy regulation and permitting requirements administered by bureaucracies, *corruption* and waste of taxpayer funds are likely. If fees/charges for public services are set at a low level, there may be incentives to privately "bid up" the price by offering officials special incentives (e.g. bribes), since the only market is political.

Corruption Scandals and Political Pricing. The term *corruption* can often mean that public officials (whether permit or contract-granting bureaucrats, regulators, service providers) gain *personal wealth* from the System 2 policy/arrangement by accepting *bribes* from businesses or individuals. This machinery is built into System 2 and the more public/state control of taxpayer money available, the more likely there is for corruption to take place. Since System 2 does not have a pricing system/market prices (to bid up the price of the contract), an effective way for businesses is to offer bribes to the officials themselves as a *political form of pricing*.

Systemic Problem. A critical point to be made here is that the politicians/officials who are embroiled in such corruption scandals are only *a symptom* of the problem, not the cause, which is the system of derivative inflows to System 2. When scandals become known, officials (or business executives) may be prosecuted and jailed for their behavior, but the problem is *systemic* in origin. This is not to categorically defend such individuals, just to point out that

if the System 2 funding for contracts exist, the ritual/public pillorying of targets does nothing to root out the fundamental source of the problem: derivative inflows and the power to grant contracts.

Bribe Payers. Those firms paying bribes in this case are not viewed as "victims" and therefore are not classified in **Col E** because they are paying a political *cost of their own (the bribe)* to the officials in exchange for some favorable treatment: A major example as already noted in **Sub1.2** is businesses trying win a contract bid; other examples include businesses trying to "buy" a regulatory loophole for their business, a zoning exemption, or a streamlining of permitting requirements. For medical patients, the bribe might be priority in line and extended service for publicly-provided medical care. A similar situation applies for preferences in *public housing*.

Public Projects. In *public housing* or *public works/infrastructural projects* where the government grants the contracts, a second source of potential *bribe* income exists for officials in charge of deciding on the awarding of contracts; construction companies may be willing to pay the decision-makers handsomely to obtain such contracts. Moreover, because of cost-decoupling (billed to taxpayers) and returns (paid to the construction companies/contractors), there is less if any incentive for financial controls, producing a distortion that allows for *inflated contract bids* and *contract overbilling* with the additional gains pocketed by the companies and possibly shared with the public officials. Also see **Sub1.2a Granting/Awarding of Contracts.**

Unjust Wealth and Wealth Inequality. Many decoupling policy interventions may be often overlooked as a possible cause of certain forms of injustice. The question of "just" and "unjust" wealth acquisition is critical; wealth obtained by means of such interventions and resulting distortions as shown in the policy tables (**Col D**) would be categorized as *unjust*. This contrasts with wealth achieved in the absence of economic distortions and obtained by serving others (e.g. selling to voluntary customers) honestly while having *full* accountability for one's actions (cost-bearing).

Qualifications. A policy that results in a concentration of wealth in favor of a group does not imply that the recipients all are becoming "rich" in an absolute sense. Those favored by policy might be *relatively* better off than without the policy intervention, and possibly are *relatively* wealthier than they would have been compared to others thanks to the intervention.

There are some cases however, when the intervention results in remarkable transfers of wealth, particularly through the expropriation and transfer of assets, whether businesses, real estate, or other property (e.g. **Sub2.2**).

Also, with regards to *redistribution* of inflows (as in **Sub1.1 and Sub1.2**), it is sometimes forgotten that some System 1 recipients may be simply receiving back *part* of the funds they had *previously paid,* minus a portion paid for the System 2 administrative handling of the wealth transfer.

Regarding **Subsystem 1 2 and 3** where inflows from System 1 pay the salaries or contract revenues of System 2 entities it may be helpful to clarify the flows and associated transfers of wealth. An example is provided below.

Example of Derivative Inflows and Wealth Transfer. To illustrate the derivative inflows, consider 4 people, three of who earn a *gross* salary of 100 currency units and who pay half of their gross in income-based fees (commonly referred to as *income taxes*); the fourth person's salary is 50 units and they do not pay any income-based fees. What is the *gross* combined salary of all four people? What is their *net* salary combined?

Frame 1. Simply summing their gross and net salaries would yield 350 and 200 as seen in the table below:

Derivative Inflows Accounting- Frame 1					
Without Netting	Person 1	Person 2	Person 3	Person 4	Total
Gross Salary	100	100	100	50	350
Income-based Fees	50	50	50	0	150
Net Salary	50	50	50	50	200

Frame 2. However, when considering the implications of a derivative inflows system (System 2), the answer may not be possible until we know what portion of the gross salary of each person originated from someone else's *income-based fees*. Person #1 and #2 earn their gross salaries in System 1. Suppose that person #3's gross salary of 100 is derived from the income-based fees of person #1 and #2, and like the others person #3 pays half of the 100 in income-based fees. Suppose that person #4, who receives only 50 units of gross salary, receives the entire 50 units that person #3 pays. Person #4 pays no income-based fees due to a graduated tax system that categorizes them as exempt due to low income.

Using arrows to show the accounting and movement of derivative inflows from System 1 to System 2 (as well within Sys2 to Sys2) it becomes apparent that combining the gross salaries of all four persons should be 200 units, which is the total of the gross salaries of Person 1 and 2 from System 1, half of which was decoupled from them and moved to System 2.

Derivative Inflows Accounting- Frame 2					
Physical Flow	System 1		System 2		
Accounting	Person 1	Person 2	Person 3	Person 4	Total
Gross Salary	100	100	100	50	350
Income-based Fees	50	50	50	0	150
Net Salary	50	50	50	50	200

Frame 3. Double-Counting Adjustment. There is a further step involved that presents the *end result* of the physical flows by adjusting for *double-counting*, as follows:

Derivative Inflows Accounting- Frame 3					
Physical Flow	System 1		System 2		
Result	Person 1	Person 2	Person 3	Person 4	Total
Gross Salary	100	100			200
Income-based Fees	50	50			100
Net Salary	50	50			100

The gross salaries combined are 200 and the net salaries are 100 since 100 of income-based fees are simply the *same* funds transferred over from System 1 to System 2.

In conclusion, the inflows of System 2 (person #3 and #4) are simply the transfers of the income-based fees from the persons in System 1.

Absence of Return. For certain policy interventions, particularly in Subsystem 2 it is also possible that due to the destruction of wealth involved in the disruption/distortion, *no financial or economic return* whatsoever accrues to *any* group; the benefit to a group might be in appearances only. (Re: *Dead-weight cost of taxes* as noted above)

Political Return. The only measurable return in such a case might be in the form of *political support* for elected public officials who promise to deliver those benefits to the group (also see *rent-seeking, vote-buying*) using the power of fiat override (re: Subsystem 2 in particular).

Transfer of Cost: Use of Policy to Economize. Businesses may attempt to rent-seeking using the System 2 machinery to push legislatively to legally *lower their costs at the expense of others* (primarily imposing this cost onto income-based payers); this too is a distortion which passes on costs involuntarily to others while the firms benefit. This intervention is a form of *cost transfer* of Subsystem 2: policy **2.5b;** many industries and scenarios are possible; the special case of the health insurance industry is detailed in **Sub1.1a**.

Cost avoidance also applies to firms seeking to lower their costs of environmental clean-up (e.g. a chemical plant that has left a toxic dump on its grounds and negotiates a deal with public officials to transfer the proper to public ownership to be cleaned up at taxpayer expense).

Column E. Decoupling: Cost portion. Cost-Bearers (those bearing the cost/burden)

A decoupling intervention that assigns, or leaves the associated cost to be borne by a group is noted here in **Col E**.

For Subsystem 1 (Redistribution), the primary decoupling intervention of income-based fees means that income-based payers bear the cost. This is reflected in a lower net income for them (*net* meaning income *after* costs) or *reduced* wealth -- *impoverishment* through the policy distortions.

In Subsystem 2, a variety of cost-bearers exist according to the nature of the intervention.

In Subsystem 3, an important cost is borne by holders of currency due to currency dilution that results from additional creation of currency units (fiat money) and declining purchasing power of the currency over time.

Column F. Rent-Seeking Activity. Col F, rent-seeking marks the beginning of the phases of feedback loops. The concept of rent-seeking is key to politics and Subsystem 2 and involves a "political" marketplace. In the economic activity as described for System 1, a business or individual attempt to provide something of value to someone else (a customer) in exchange for money (or something else).

Rent seekers attempt to gain (increase wealth) by providing no goods or services in exchange, other than their vote and support. Subsystem 2 allows this to occur because of its power to override the decisions and actions of others, as well as bypassing the judicial system. Therefore rent-seekers can "sell" their votes to put an official (lawmaker, politician) in power who can "buy" their votes with their overriding authority. The result is law and regulations that can furnish certain groups (the rent-seekers) with advantages over others. Some of these advantages are detailed in the Sub2 table.

From a feedback loop perspective, rent-seeking may have its own reinforcing feedback loop cycle: Companies suffering from lower returns due to poor management or worsening market conditions may seek policy interventions to maintain their market share/profits and to reduce competition. However, this political maneuvering causes the companies to be focused less on market conditions/consumer demand and more on *political action* -- this can result in progressively lower revenues for these very companies, inducing them to *further* resort to political measures. Meanwhile, competitors lobby for market-opening (deregulation) measures in opposition to this feedback loop.

Column G. Impaired Production and Reduced Income Impacts: If the policy causes a financial entity such as a business or self-employed individual to lower production (do less business) and lower income, this column applies. Transfer payments generate an incentive to lower income to benefit from low-income status, increasing the burden on the cost-bearers. As the feedback loop progresses, the eventual result in the overshoot is income insufficient to cover expenditures of the system.

Column H. Shortages (including Food Crises). Shortages of goods and/or services normally provided by Sys1 financial entities. This can include *labor shortages* due to certain policies described in **Sub2.4**. In extreme cases, policy-induced food shortages can result in famine (**Sub2.1a, Sub2.2b**). These policies can include actions during armed conflicts preventing producers from getting their goods to consumers leading to malnutrition/famine; this in combination with repeated shelling, plumbing, sewage, and public sanitation systems may be destroyed, contaminating water supplies, and contributing to the outbreak of disease (see **Sub2.6a**).

Shortages can also arise in the provision of various services that are in the domain of the public sector (System 2). Some examples include *public housing* and *socialized medicine* or *public health care*. These services are funded by income-based fees (taxes) and generally provided to people at a low (or zero) cost to users with the aim of assisting low-income households and the needy. There is a risk that there will be greater demand for the service than the supply available because as economic theory suggests, the lower the price at which something is offered, the greater the quantity that will tend to be demanded. Offering at a lower price than would otherwise be possible if costs were truly reflected understandably attracts users of the service. In the medical area, shortages can be seen in longer wait times for various procedures, and less attention by overworked doctors. In such circumstances, desperate patients and their families may try to "compensate" their doctors and surgeons in the form of *bribes* to be given priority (also see **Col D** in the context of *corruption* and wealth gain for public officials). As noted there, bribes are a type of "political" pricing mechanism when a market pricing system is absent.

Public Works and Corruption. Also see a particularly lucrative form of non-market pricing in the discussion regarding **Col D Wealth Gains**, in which both public officials and contractors can gain handsomely from *bribes, inflated bids,* and *overbilling issues.* In public housing, construction companies hired to do these public housing projects can benefit from wealth gains at taxpayer expense, as well as in some instances, public officials who may be offered (and accept) special remuneration (bribes) for priority access to certain housing units, etc.
Also see **Sub1.2a Granting/Awarding of Contracts.**

Funding Difficulties. More specific to public housing, the funds for housing projects compete with other System 2 activities including *transfer payments*; therefore, it is not always possible to secure the amount of funding necessary to provide the level of housing/apartments demanded at the (low) price offered (including a price of *zero).* In addition to the time-consuming need to lobby for funding, the bureaucratic processes, construction time and administration of the housing program itself are particularly demanding. With tight budgets, System 2 entities might over time tend to gravitate towards less administratively cumbersome processes of helping the needy through simple welfare payments and/or housing allowances.

Column I. Black Markets/Violence due to contract illegality: Black markets can sometimes also be also referred to as *free* or *unregulated markets** although the specifics must be examined. Black markets tend to develop when some form of intervention (whether concerning ownership, regulation, or outright bans/prohibition) prevents satisfaction of demand, meaning that there are willing buyers for the good, service or labor.
***Note:** When official data is unavailable or suppressed, *black market data* can be instrumental in deriving estimates. In the case of inflation estimates: "As long as there is an active black market (read: free market) for currency and the black-market data are available, changes in the black-market exchange rate can be

reliably transformed into accurate estimates of countrywide inflation rates. The economic principle of Purchasing Power Parity (PPP) allows for this transformation." (Hanke 2017: Re: *purchasing power parity* PPP; Venezuela 2017)

Major policies giving rise to black markets are noted here:
Services/Activities: Sub2.3a (e.g. prostitution)
Labor: See **Sub2.4c** (also relates to *services*: If the labor were legal, the legal business activity associated with providing labor to employers would be a personnel service or temporary agency). *Human trafficking* can relate to both **Sub2.3a, Sub2.4c**.
Product/Goods Bans/Prohibition (example: illegal drugs): See **Sub2.6**. The violence associated with prohibition and product bans is of concern: Because these products are illegal, there is no legal way to purchase or enforce a geographic or territorial claim for distribution of the product. Therefore, to enforce the claim, violence is resorted to. For further detail, see **Sub2.6**.
Bans on private property ownership **(Re: Sub2.2** *central planning* and **Sub2.2b)** also can give rise to black markets. A case in point might be the former Soviet Union and other centrally-planned economies that heavily restrict or ban private property. Although official government stores exist, a large underground economy (black market) also exists to provide goods and services outside of the centrally-planned system.
High level of Decoupling (Taxation). Some countries permitting private ownership may impose very high levels of taxation (more than 70-80% for certain income brackets, for example) so that a black market of bartering may develop for those most affected such as high-income earners (e.g. dentist trades services with a doctor).

Column J. Clustering: Oversupply, Excessive Speculation, and Competition (Simultaneous Error). Oversupply can also be referred to as a "glut." In Subsystem 2. policies governing pricing and subsidization that may cause a higher risk of oversupplies of goods (and possibly some services) are indicated here.

Excessive speculation arises from a desperate search for yield when due to *financial repression* or *inflationary environments* where savers attempt to earn higher (and potentially much *riskier* returns on their money). High inflation can cause investors to protect the value of their savings by investing in stock and other asset markets, pushing up asset prices leading to *bubbles*.

Excessive (cut-throat) competition also may result from oversupply (gluts) that also believed to have policy origins either coming from (1) pricing policies/controls (See **Sub2.1a, Sub2.2c**; where prices are set too high in relationship to costs), often coupled with subsidization; or (2) monetary policies and the dynamics of Subsystem 3 that artificially lowers the cost of borrowing and distort incentives to produce with *more debt* than otherwise (Re: debt accumulation). A likely outcome is that entrepreneurs/businesses *overproduce* and oversupply the market leading to unsold inventories (also re: *excess capacity*) and subsequent (cash flow) losses when too much product floods the market, forcing down prices and leaving too little cash flow to repay the excessive debt overhang (Re: fiat money creation; fractional reserve banking; Austrian business cycle theory).

Clustering Behavior Dynamics. The defining feature here is that the *same error* is made almost simultaneously; this is expected to have origins in policy and some form of centralized planning (many entities following the same signal), and tends to precede or may nearly coincide with the **Overshoot (Col K)** and secondary policies in response (**Col L**) next.

Column K. Overshoot: Deficit/Debt (Expenditures>Inflows): When System 2 administrative units face a higher risk of spending (expenditures) exceeding inflows because of a given policy, the elevated risk of **deficits and debt accumulation** is indicated as a "1" in this column.

This is an overshoot phase which can also be described as a *fiscal crisis* of a given administrative unit in Sys2; this phase is believed to be the product of feedback loops of prior policy interventions, to varying degrees.

Note that for **Subsystem 3** (fiat money), the overshoot problem concerns *income being insufficient to repay debt*. While money creation is deployed to cover deficits and repay debt, at a certain overshoot phase, the increased quantities of money can lead to elevated inflation rates, and in extreme cases, hyperinflations, with consequences as seen in subsequent columns.

Orphaned (Decoupled) Funds and Leakage. A critical underpinning of this overshoot whereby expenditures exceed inflows is termed *leakage,* and which is an inherent component of the feedback loop of System 2. Again, the act of *involuntary cost-decoupling* (costs borne by System 1 actors with (all or part of) the returns transferred to System 2) sets in motion a flow of funds that lose rightful *ownership*.

Public Funds and Accountability. As *public funds* are largely *costless* to the System 2 users, there is less incentive for accountability as there is no clear title to the funds or incentive to use them to economize on resources (Re: General Accounting Office GAO of the United States; Audits). Both overuse and misuse of funds typically describe *leakage*: The use of funds in anticipation of continued funding in the future with a certain portion of the orphaned funds becoming "lost" and no longer accounted for, as audits can sometimes discover.

This is not to say that embezzlement, theft and "lost" funds do not occur anywhere. The difference is believed to be in the level of incentives *against* leakage within System 1.

Column L. Secondary Policies / Impacts (including extra-judicial actions/ state violence)

Secondary *impacts* of policies, or policies (or *policy responses*) as *by-products of an initial policy* are numerous. Some principal types are noted in the tables, including *crackdowns*, controls (prices, wages), rationing, social welfare expansion, and prosecutions. State violence may be a marked feature of this stage.

Phase 1 Delay 2. As for deregulations, asset sales, privatizations, and *austerity measures**, these are expected to be part of the

Phase 1 Delay 2 *reversal phase* following the overshoot. Other variations can be public-private partnerships to run facilities, ports, highways, and other infrastructure previously operated within Sys2.

(*) **Note: Austerity measures** refers to secondary policies (**Col L**) following the overshoot phase (**Col K**) that include budget cutbacks, tax increases, reductions of benefits and subsidies, and means-testing for recipients of certain welfare benefits. Reductions of benefits can generate particularly volatile social backlashes as noted in Column N.

Crackdowns on an activity are a common secondary policy response as a by-product of an initial policy intervention. The type of crackdown varies according to the type of policy, and often centers on black markets that have developed in response to the distortions that the policies have created in Sys1.

While **prosecutions** may be processed through the court system, the initial impetus for the prosecution may come from a policy response.

Continuity. A particularly serious concern regarding crackdowns is not only the violence that can occur, but also the belief that following the crackdown, the problem has been resolved. Because the problem has a policy origin, the potential for continued crackdowns –and future violence—remains.

Column M. Heightened Ownership Insecurity (including self-ownership); Hoarding. Certain interventions may cause businesses and individuals to fear losing something into which they have invested resources (time and money). This can also include a *regulation* that can adversely impact upon future revenues or profitability for the business, or a massive *fine/penalty* that generates losses and can even threaten the financial viability of the firm.

Insecurity of self-ownership refers to the individual's own security and freedom of movement or choice. Hoarding and the concealment of goods and various forms of wealth can also be a reaction to a perceived threat to one's future security.

Budget Cuts and Security. In the overshoot, fiscal crises and cost-cutting measures can result in reductions of law enforcement personnel, leading to increased ownership insecurity. This can sometimes be offset by System 1 contracting with private security services. As is seen below in **Col N**, secondary policies, it is also possible that *crackdowns* on suspected offenders (those ignoring policies, protesters against certain policies, etc.) may lead to a wider sense of unease regarding personal safety.

When benefits and subsidies are reduced in a reversal phase it is understandable that recipients will perceive this as a loss of ownership (even though the benefits may actually be *redistributed* benefits from others), and may react to the loss in the form of protest and social unrest (**Col N**). When public finances begin to worsen, as part of austerity measures (noted above in **Col L**), officials may attempt tax hikes to increase inflows to Sys2; heightening public perception of ownership insecurity in terms of their reduced net take home pay and increased cost of living.

Column N. Visible Protests/Unrest: Protests (discontent, social unrest) in themselves may be the result of perceived or real injustices. Unrest may be silent as certain groups may be angered by the actions of authorities or impacts of a new policy or regulation but not visibly express it. There are certain instances when the outbursts of discontent can be explosive --when certain benefits (including subsidies, preferential tax treatment, or even *removal* of punitive tax treatment) previously bestowed upon certain groups are suddenly modified.

Protest/unrest can also be the result of a *delayed* feedback loop -- System 2 cost-cutting measures when financial problems begin to mount in an administrative unit (also see **Column F**).

Non-Prosecution. A critical source of potential future conflict is detailed in **Sub2.5c-judicial immunity** when local communities, ethnic or religious groups and individuals are the victim of persecution and violence including rape by the authorities, their supporters, or others, but have no reliable recourse in the courts (which refuse to hear the cases or which are perceived as biased; Re: judicial bias) due to possible influence of the ruling party in swaying court decisions. Members of the persecuted groups may either flee or turn to violence, including joining existing rebel or insurgent groups for support. (On conflict also see Fellman, et al. 2016).

Another possible case involves black market operators (e.g. smugglers) whose activities have *benefited from a previous policy environment*. Legalization/liberalization policies can give rise to considerable opposition and backlashes. For example, policies *reducing* tariffs (import taxes) on goods pose a threat to the smugglers by reducing (tax-included) prices of the *legal* tax-paying operators and creating more competition for the smugglers who previously benefited by undercutting the high *legal* prices. For details also see the interventions of **Sub2.6.**

SUBSYSTEM 1: Derivative Inflows and Redistribution

The following subsystem and policy table summarizes the characteristics of Subsystem 1 (Sub1) of System 2. Highlights and historical examples will be noted where possible. Abbreviations are as follows: **Sub1.4a** means Subsystem 1, policy 4a; **Sub2.4a Col B** refers to column B of Subsystem 1 policy 4a. The subsystem and policy tables are also abbreviated *policy tables*.

Non-fiat element refers to administrative units that do not have a central bank at their disposal. This typically applies to municipalities, counties, states, prefectures, provinces, etc. below the national (or if nation-state central banks are superseded by a supranational state central bank), then the supranational, level.

The fiat money element comes into play as an addition financing tool (source of inflows) in Subsystem 3 to be discussed further below.

Subsystem 1 Policy Table. The policy table for subsystem 1 is shown here, broken into two major parts: First, basic *information* of each policy in Columns A through E including the beneficiaries (wealth transfer) and cost-bearers; second, the *phases* (Initial, overshoot, reversal) in Columns F through N.

SUBSYSTEM 1 of System 2

I. REDISTRIBUTION OF DERIVATIVE INFLOWS (with fiat law adjustments; Financing: Initially non-fiat via taxes, bonds)

Sub1.#	A. POLICY INTERVENTION TYPE	B. Level/Scale (primary)	C. Rhetorical Justification (Also: Ideology)	D. Decoupling: Returns portion. Wealth gains via political support. (Income/wealth distorted upwards)	E. Decoupling : Cost portion. Cost-Bearers: bearing the cost (Net incomes/wealth reduced)
Sub1.1	Transfer Payments*/Other Unearned Benefits	All	Fairness/Morality	Individuals	Sys 1 income-based payers (=taxpayers)
	*including universal basic income (UBI) and "pay-as-you-go" pensions.				
	a. Special case: Insurance (health, disaster, etc.)			See Sub 1.4a, Sub2.5b	Sys 1 income-based payers
Sub1.2	Granting/Awarding of Contracts	All	Growth/Security	Recipients/firms*	Sys 1 income-based payers
	a. Non-recognition of equity/debt ownership of taxpayers.			*incl. reduced cost of financing	
Sub1.3	Employee compensation of Sys2 entities	All	Growth/Security	Recipients	Sys 1 income-based payers
	a. Non-recognition of equity/debt ownership of taxpayers.				
Sub1.4	Compensation to Producers/Corporate Welfare	All	Growth/Security	Recipients	Sys 1 income-based payers
	a. Subsidization of firms/Industry (incl. export subsidies)			Favored industry	Producers of subsidized im
	b. Subsidies for consumer goods (via producers)			Merchants, Consumers	Sys 1 income-based payers
	c. Bailouts to firms for losses/corporate welfare (Also see Sub3.4)			Firms; bondholders	Sys 1 income-based payers
Sub1.5	Income-based Fee (Tax) Reductions without commensurate expenditure reductions.	All	Growth/Security	Beneficiaries	Excluded groups
				Favored enties/individua	Sys 1 income-based payers
Sub1.6	Foreign Aid (Funds or Goods)	Natl/Supranatil	Fairness/Morality	Favored entities; officials	Sys1 Income-based payers

SUBSYSTEM 1 of System 2

SUBSYSTEM 1 PHASES: Hypothesized elevated risk of occurrence (including delayed impacts)

I. REDISTRIBUTION OF DERIVATIVE INFLOWS—Cont'd

Sub.1.#	A. POLICY INTERVENTION TYPE	Phase 1 (Initial)					Delay 1-Overshoot	Delay 2-Reversal		
		F. Rent-seeking activity	G. Impaired Production/Reduced Income Impacts	H. Shortages (incl. Food crises)	I. Black markets/violence due to contract non-legality	J. Clustering Oversupply/ excess. Spec. and competition	K. Deficit/Debt (Expenddb Inflows)	L. Secondary Policies / Impacts (incl. extra-judicial/ state violence)	M. Ownership insecurity (incl. self); hoarding	N. Visible protests/ unrest
Sub1.1	Transfer Payments*/Other Unearned Benefits	1					1	Cuts, means testing	After cuts	After cuts
	*including universal basic income (UBI) and "pay-as-you-go" pensions.									
	a. Special case: Insurance (health, disaster, etc.)	1					1			
Sub1.2	Granting/Awarding of Contracts	1					1			
	a. Non-recognition of equity/debt ownership of taxpayers.									
Sub1.3	Employee compensation of Sys2 entities	1					1	Outsourcing		After cuts
	a. Non-recognition of equity/debt ownership of taxpayers.									
Sub1.4	Compensation to Producers/Corporate Welfare	1				1	1	Crackdown		
	a. Subsidization of firms/Industry (incl. export subsidies)	1								
	b. Subsidies for consumer goods (via producers)			1*	1		1	Crackdowns, cuts		After cuts
	c. Bailouts to firms for losses/corporate welfare (Also see Sub.3.4)	1	1*	*depends on policy specifics						
Sub1.5	Income-based Fee (Tax) Reductions without commensurate expenditure reductions.	1	*through zombification				1	Crackdowns	After hikes	After increases
Sub1.6	Foreign Aid (Funds or Goods)	1	1		1					See text

Subsystem 1 Column Detail

Col C. The wealth transfer can be directed towards countless types of recipients, as well as consumers of select goods and favored businesses.

Col F. Rent-seeking is a dominant activity to receive some of the redistributed inflows. Note that budgets may distinguish between *discretionary* and *non-discretionary*. Non-discretionary expenditures such as pension fund obligations, medical coverage for the elderly (e.g. Medicare) in the United States, and interest payments on the national debt are not expected to be subject to budget cuts and over time may take an increasing share of the budget, forcing reductions in *discretionary* programs.

Sub1.1 Transfer Payments/Other Benefits

Transfer payments are redistributions of money sourced typically from income-based payers (taxpayers). These payments can be defined as a "one-way payment to a person for which no money, good or service is given or exchanged." (Investopedia) Many such programs exist. Examples are: Social benefit programs, (social) welfare, low-income assistance, health care payment assistance, pensions/social security, disability payments, grants (student, research etc.) and unemployment compensation. Two areas of focus are pension/social security (*pay-as-you-go* systems) and health care payment assistance. Transfer payments paid to business entities broadly called *corporate welfare* and including *subsidies* are dealt with separately in **Sub1.4.**

Pension Systems. Pension systems vary, but simplifying, there are two basic forms (1) invested (2) pay-as-you-go (PAYG). The PAYG system is classified here as part of Sub1's redistribution.

Invested pension systems invest the payments into system by employees (which can be either System 1 or System 2 individuals) for their future retirement into funds with actual invested assets such as stocks and bonds. (2) In the pay-as-you-go (PAYG) system, the payments/contributions made are not invested, but rather, are made immediately available to the government for *current* expenditures and are not invested. One source of confusion is that PAYG systems *do* have assets but these assets may simply be *obligations to pay* (I.O.U.s) to the pension system from the Treasury or Finance Ministry. For the legal basis of the PAYG system in U.S., see Helvering v. Davis, 301 U.S. 619 (1937): (Mitchell 2017a).

Universal basic income (UBI) or *unconditional income* has become an experimental form of transfer payment in various countries that differ from standard unemployment benefits in that the recipients do not need to show proof of need. While the benefits of the system are lower stress and improved well-being as reported by recipients and proponents, the longer-term impacts on country finances are not generally addressed; estimates in the case of Finland suggest increased government deficits of about 5% of GDP (Chapman 2017; Bregman 2017). Moreover, if the reinforcing feedback loop dynamic remains unresolved, such well-intended programs could in an overshoot phase result in budget cuts, leaving many dependent households and individuals stranded (**Sub1.1 Col L**)

Although a linkage between fiat crypto-assets and UBI may not be currently obvious, it is possible that (despite the *extreme* risk of loss and volatility), some fiat cryptocurrencies and alt-coins might be proposed or increasingly used as a supplemental source of income through (hoped-for) appreciation in value/increased purchasing power. **Sub3.6b** addresses crypto-assets which are *not* viewed as policy-originated per se, but as an extension of traditional central bank fiat money.

Sub1.1a
Disaster Insurance (Floods, storms). Taxpayer-funded insurance programs or subsidies for residents in zones that are at high risk of natural disasters (floods, storms, etc.) are made available for families in need. A concern is whether the *lowered costs* (due to subsidies) and/or future potential *insurance payouts* could encourage families to intentionally put themselves in harm's way by *living in and/or returning* to these known high-risk areas. If an artificial incentive is being created to lower the cost of living in a dangerous area and exposing them to danger once again, the

policy should be reconsidered to prevent dangerous and fatal outcomes due to such distorted incentives.

Health Insurance: Detail. A more complex variant of transfer payments involves the system of *third party payments* whereby an entity legally or contractually interposes themselves between consumers and providers of the service. As a result, instead of the patient paying the doctor *directly*, the third party pays for (all or part of) the medical services rendered. The third-party payer can be: 1. an agency of government (typically for low-income households or seniors) or 2. private health insurance companies.

Individuals pay regular health insurance premiums in hopes of having adequate coverage, especially in the case of catastrophic medical bills. For low-income or senior households that receive so-called "free" healthcare plans paid for by government agencies, households may pay a small or no premium; income-based payers (taxpayers) are then the source of the funds to pay the doctors.

Summary and Analysis. System 1 would normally be characterized by voluntary contractual arrangements for third-party payment of the service, i.e. private health insurance providers. In System 2, health insurance premiums and medical services are expected to be (all or in part) paid for by *income-based* payers (i.e. taxpayers) through redistribution; **Sub1.1a** applies to this portion. There is however, a significant complication involving private health insurance providers to be discussed in the analysis below.

Analysis of 1.1a. Col D. As previously noted in the Column D detail as well as later in the discussion of **Sub2.5b**, firms can be expected to use System 2 machinery to legally *lower their costs* at the expense of others. Health insurance companies, can use legislative means to pass on the medical costs onto income-based payers (taxpayers). Moreover, as discussed in **Sub2.5e**, legal coverage mandates (be covered or pay a fine) benefit health insurance company revenues by fiat law.

The analysis of unfair wealth transfer to the insurance companies is complex. In some cases, there is a clear source of wealth concentration, including the health insurance providers in the form of legal reduction of costs and legal purchasing requirements, and the medical community (e.g. physicians, hospitals, pharmaceutical companies, medical equipment suppliers, etc.) in the form of additional income to them, both potentially at taxpayer expense. However, the benefit to the insurance companies needs to be seen from two perspectives:

(1) If the firms' action is in response to *prior* legislation requiring the firms to cover *pre-existing conditions* and *uninsurable risks* (e.g. a patient who they were forced *by law* to cover that is costing them several million dollars annually) the "benefit" of a lowered cost is not one that they would have opted to bear in the first place;

(2) If the firm had covered an individual who later required inordinately expensive medical treatments, *actuarially* speaking the firm should have been able to adjust for this (keeping revenues and actuarial costs in line) with health insurance premiums from healthy contributors probabilistically paying for the others. In this case, should the firms try to drop the patients and legally pass their costs onto taxpayers, this should clearly appear in **Col D** as an *unfair* benefit to the firm. The line item for the policy itself is **Sub2.5b** (regulations and legal preferences to *transfer costs* onto others).

Over time, the following outcomes within the healthcare industry may be likely: A decrease in the proportion of total medical costs being paid directly to the medical service providers by individuals/households themselves and more by taxpayers (in other words, a declining proportion of *self-financing* of these costs); a *cost-shifting* in which households at certain income levels* bearing a *greater proportion* of healthcare costs than those in other income strata.

Middle to middle-high income earners might be more likely to bear a higher proportion than the poor or the highest income or low-income brackets.

It is hoped that for a given quality of care that medical costs continue to fall so that eventually patients and insurers are longer run the risk of being bankrupted by treatments (Re: medical bankruptcy)

Calls for *universal health care* or *single payer* may be well-intentioned means to solve the problem of inadequate coverage (with perhaps some hope to reduce healthcare costs). However, the problems of cost containment in medicine and health care may remain; depending on complex legislative details, this adjustment could add *additional* impetus to the reinforcing feedback loop and eventual overshoot (leading to potential default for the related System 2 entities e.g. Medicaid and Medicare in the U.S.) as the cost burden shifts increasingly to income-based payers (taxpayers). Afterwards, there may be a forced system-wide push towards cost-cutting of which the consequences for those receiving care at that time a major concern.

Therefore, the emphasis on economization leading to natural lowering of costs is preferable. Although apples-to-apples comparisons may not always be possible, comparison between the *speed of cost reductions* for various procedures might be informative: For example, secular declines in costs of third-party payer-insured/subsidized surgical procedures vs. *uninsured direct-payment* surgeries (e.g. cosmetic surgeons).

The impetus for economizing on costs is still expected to continue (albeit perhaps slower than desired). Improved public health, hygiene and basic sanitation practices and awareness, combined with path-breaking technological advancements in medicine including preventive medicine, diagnostics, low-cost vaccines, and genome-editing technologies (Re: CRISPR/Cas9, Clustered Regularly Interspaced Short Palindromic Repeats) can help with the fight against pathogens and many kinds of diseases and disorders. It is hoped that progress in these areas will be able to meet the needs of those needing care during and following a possible overshoot phase.

Sub1.2 Granting/Awarding of Contracts (combined with Sub1.2a)

Artificially Lowered Cost of Capital. Under current accounting practices (Generally Accepted Accounting Practices or GAAP), taxpayer funds used to pay firms with contracts are treated as "revenues" and are not recognized as investment capital (either equity or debt capital) for the firm. This could be described as a form of *corporate welfare* and *crony capitalism* (see above in the **Col C** discussion) that gives the firms a *lower cost of capital* (financing cost) than would be the case if the ownership of taxpayer funds were properly accounted for and the firms were accountable to taxpayer-investors in the same way that they are accountable to investors. Proper accounting would allow for taxpayers to receive a return on their (taxed) capital.

Understandably, a variety of industries are likely to vie for contracts as this is their business and governments can be major customers for them. These include contractors/construction companies, some food suppliers and distributors, and defense/aerospace, to name a few. The contracts are granted for various purposes including public investment/infrastructure, public works and housing projects, and defense and national security. The importance of security is not in question here, but rather the potential for inflated costs, waste and accountability due to the decoupling process and non-recognition of taxpayer ownership (**Sub1.2a**).

Contracts granted for the purpose of public investment and infrastructure-building policies in which contracts are granted to construction companies and developers are an important element of policies ostensibly for growth and development. However, there is generally a misconception regarding public infrastructure spending that it should *precede* economic activity as a form of *stimulus* for development. In fact, infrastructure is naturally more likely to be built *in the course of* the development process. The 20th century historical record suggests a poor record of public investment policy in developing countries (Bauer 1984:248;

Abramovitz 1956; Cairncross 1962; Denison 1974; Kuznets 1966: 80-81 as cited by Bauer; Solow 1957). On developing economies also see Myint (1980).

Sub1.2a Non-recognition of equity/debt ownership of taxpayers (see above **Sub1.2** general commentary).

Sub1.3 Direct Employment/Compensation: After the overshoot and in a reversal phase, it is possible that *budget cuts* are sought and public employees are replaced by contract employees and certain functions outsourced to various organizations.

Sub1.4. Compensation to Producers/Corporate Welfare

Sub1.4a. Subsidization of Firms/Industry

Subsidization of a given type of production gives the appearance of stimulating an industry or desirable activity. However, as costs of subsidization are borne by taxpayers, the distortion and feedback loop involved produce unintended effects—including the *opposite* of what was intended. Subsidization often works in conjunction with *price controls*, covered in **Sub2.1a** and in further detail in Appendix 1.

The subsidization encourages the industry to increase supply, but the result of the increased supply, absent a commensurate increase in demand, is often a *decline in the price* of the good. Because of the popularity of the lower prices, it is likely for the policy to continue encouraging increased supply to the point that prices fall to levels that not only discourage further production, but that can *cause producers to be unable to cover their costs of production*, causing a stoppage of industry production! Eventually when this reinforcing feedback loop plays itself out in failure, the subsidy may be scaled back or halted.

Subsidies in Renewable Energy Policymaking. An easily overlooked result of *controlled prices* in energy should be pointed out. Suppose that well-meaning policymakers set the price of *renewable* energy sources higher than non-renewable, traditional energy sources to encourage renewable energy use (such as solar energy). While the idea seems sound, the results can be wasteful and are summarized as follows:

1. **Consumption.** This discourages use of renewable energy sources because their controlled price is set higher, *unless* subsidized by the taxpayers. If subsidized, the price is potentially lowered to the point of *energy overuse*, even if from renewable sources.

3. **Production and Artificial Cost Differential**

This gives firms an artificial incentive to use *more* of the *lower cost* energy source and produce more of the legally higher-priced renewable energy. Putting these two together, renewable energy production can be increased by *using* the lower controlled price as an input and locking in a return based on the difference between the controlled prices. How? For example, by shining light (using regular energy at the *lower* cost) onto solar panels at night. Then the solar energy generated this way can be sold at the higher, controlled price. Because this may be subsidized, the taxpayers bear the cost, consumer energy overuse may be encouraged, and the firm receives the return from the controlled cost differential.

Health Insurance. Health insurance costs for qualified low-income customers (U.S.) may also be subsidized. The subsidy is paid to the insurer (health insurance companies) to improve the affordability of the cost of health insurance. The firms receive a wealth transfer from taxpayers there is a benefit to the low-income consumers of their services as well--a form of redistribution funded by taxpayers. The feedback loop of subsidization suggests that the lowered costs via subsidization encourage greater numbers of low-income applicants for insurance but *if further funding for subsidization is unable to match the (increased) quantity demanded*, shortages are likely to develop as insurers potentially curtail or discontinue services (Also see **Sub2.5b**).

Export subsidies provide gains to the home-country producers at the expense of home-country taxpayers and foreign producers of competing goods who face competition from more supply than would have occurred without the subsidies; these policies' adverse impacts on lifting developing nations out of poverty may lead to pressures for this this type of policy to be scaled down or eliminated.

Sub1.4b. Subsidies for consumer goods

Subsidizing consumer staples such as bread, for example, is popular with the public because consumers generally desire lower prices –however, rather than through *economization*, subsidies keep the cost of the staples artificially low with the cost borne by the taxpayers. Continuity is possible as long as producers are compensated for their losses if the subsidized prices are too low to cover their costs (or *opportunity costs* – see Appendix 1).

The unintended consequences include: The potential for a black market to emerge whereby entrepreneurial individuals capture a spread (margin) on the resale of the item by buying in one area and selling it at a higher price elsewhere; shortages can arise in certain locales when the subsidized price is held too low, leaving shelves bare while in other areas the goods are sold elsewhere at higher black-market prices. As is seen in **Col L**, crackdowns on the black-market operators are considered likely at some point in the feedback loop.

Understandably, there is considerable political pressure to continue increasing the subsidy. This type of policy can eventually place a potentially serious financial burden on the public coffers; potential for massive unrest following the overshoot phase when the government finances cannot further support the policy. Moreover, corrections in pricing are not fluid because the subsidy is set by policy (law), so that adjustments do not easily respond to market conditions. In the final phase, such programs may be scaled back or eliminated due to these unintended consequences. See Brown (1977) regarding the costs and consequences of food grain and other subsidies; further detail on the nature of subsidization is found in Appendix 1. For an example of subsidies of energy resources, see **Sub1.4a** above.

Sub1.4c. Bailouts to firms for losses

This category is related to corporate welfare, **Sub1.4a** (subsidization), **Sub3.2** (loan guarantees) and **Sub3.4** (asset purchases) because all involve special System 2 privileges granted to businesses and/or their investors. Subsystem 3 involves fiat money, but it is possible that bailouts are *also* at least partially financed with fiat money; therefore, this category may straddle both subsystems depending on the nature of the financing (non-fiat vs. fiat money).

Although not necessarily clear in news reports, in many cases bailouts of firms, banks or even governments (Re: too-big-to fail banks; bailout of Greece) involves rescuing (bailing out) *bondholders* (or in some cases stockholders). A System 2 entity, (government agency or in conjunction with central banks) will purchase the bonds of those entities at *inflated prices* (inflated in the sense that they are bought above market price; the sale of the securities on the market would have resulted in massive losses for the investors). Through rent-seeking, the bondholders, many of which may be financial institutions, intend to mitigate their losses through bail-outs; this policy-based protection from bad lending practices can create perverse incentives (economic distortions) that perpetuate bad lending practices and a reinforcing feedback loop that encourages future non-performing loans. Some forecast that in the next overshoot central banks will be unable to bail out the system, leading not to an *S-Curve* or a *reversal*, but a collapse and subsequent reset, possibly following a period of repression (e.g. martial law); see Rickards 2017. Also, re: *moral hazard*; Stockman 2013, 2016.

In sum, the totality of System 2 policy-based privileges for firms within all the subsystems including corporate welfare, subsidies, bailouts (See **Sub1**) judicial immunity, regulatory protections, legal restrictions on competition (See **Sub2**); fiat money financing and low interest rates (See **Sub3**) can benefit firms, their owners, and creditors while the costs are borne by taxpayers (income-based payers) and savers/holders of fiat currency. This also contributes to the rise of what might be loosely termed *zombie firms* (*corporate zombies*) and widespread *economic zombification* (Andrews, et al. 2017). For accounts of zombie firms in Japan (Re: Toshiba) see Chi (2017) and in Europe, see Shedlock (2017).

Sub1.5 Income-based fee reductions

Income-based fee reductions are also referred to as *tax loopholes*. An example is the *mortgage interest deduction*; not only do the borrowers potentially reduce their taxes, but the real estate and financial industry may benefit from additional home sales and home loans. Special arrangements such as *tax holidays* may also be offered to businesses for investing in some manner towards the qualified development of a specified zone.

In **Sub1.5 Col E** it may be unclear why Sys1 income-based payers are listed as bearing the cost, since taxes are being *reduced*. The reason is that it is likely that tax reductions are not typically accompanied by a *concomitant decline in spending* by System 2 entities. This means that the *same amount* of income-based fees (taxes) will now potentially be spread amongst *a smaller base* of taxpayers-- those who *do not benefit* from the tax reduction.

Note in the **Column N** general commentary the special case of acts of protest tax *reductions* on goods by smugglers who face greater competition from lower prices on those goods.

Sub1.6. Foreign Aid. The topic of redistribution through foreign aid is vast and is only briefly addressed here. Careful study may be required to determine the eventual beneficiaries of foreign aid packages and the longer-term consequences. Although the term "foreign" and "aid" suggest that foreigners, and specifically, poor people are benefiting from the policy, an analysis of the flow of funds may reveal that a significant portion of the "foreign" aid may simply be grants to *home-country contractors* for foreign-based projects, therefore this form of redistribution is essentially part of category **Sub1.2 Granting/Awarding of Contracts.** (Re: Perkins, 2005, 2016).

There is generally widespread support for *emergency* food aid or medical assistance. However, it may not be clear when the situation is no longer an emergency and when the emergency aid should end. Analysis of a Sahelian aid package (U.S. $7.5 billion) in the 1970s, revealed that the food aid became *self-perpetuating*, suggesting that even *post-crisis* local means of producing food did not develop or, if so, the food supplies were somehow diverted and resold while more aid was being requested.

Questions to be answered would include:

What was the trajectory and destination of food supplies; Who was responsible for the distribution and transfers at each stage?

Were *causes** of the food (humanitarian) crises addressed? Would the continued (post crisis) supply of food aid prevent local production and markets from developing over time?

(*For proximate causes, see **Col G**--impaired production impacts; also, **Sub2.2b** and historical research on policy in agriculture (Economist 1983; Shultz 1978).

SUBSYSTEM 2: **Fiat Law- Other Overriding Interventions**

As previously noted, legislation can give rise to *fiat laws* that override previous laws, contractual arrangements, and the decisions of others. Rent-seekers may work with lawmakers/politicians or other officials to construct fiat laws to their advantage, leading to possible wealth concentration as detailed in **Col D**.

Subsystem 2 Policy Table. The policy table below summarizes the characteristics of Subsystem 2 of System 2 (Sub2). The table is divided into two major parts: First, the basic information of each policy in Columns A through E including the beneficiaries of wealth transfer and cost-bearers; second, the phases (Initial, overshoot, reversal) in Columns F through N. Abbreviations are as follows: **Sub2.3a** means Subsystem 2, policy 3a; **Sub2.3a Col D** refers to column D of Subsystem 2 policy 3a.

SUBSYSTEM 2 of System 2

II. FIAT LAW (OTHER) WITH OVERRIDING INTERVENTIONS (Regulatory, Policy)

Sub2.#	A. POLICY INTERVENTION TYPE	B. Level/Scale (primary)	C. Rhetorical Justification	D. Decoupling: Returns portion. Wealth gains via political support. (Income/wealth distorted upwards)	E. Decoupling : Cost portion. Cost-Bearers: bearing the cost (Net incomes/wealth reduced)
Sub2.1	**Price Controls**				
⊙	a. Price or Quantity controls (caps)	All	Fairness/Morality	Exempt firms,* elected officials; Apt. renters	Impacted firms/farmers Consumers, RE owners
	b. Foreign exchange rates/currency controls (see Sub3.5b)			*for substitute goods	*RE: real estate
	c. Special Case: Control of Information (perception management)		Various	aries: Political; Private Ga	Various
Sub2.2	**Prop. Ownership Interventions/Central Planning (See Sub2.4d)**	National	Fairness/Morality	Leadership (new/old)	
⊙	a. Expropriations/seizures/transfers; land reforms		Fairness, Security	Inner Circle/supporters	Impacted owners
⊙	b. Private property bans; forced communal ownership			Competing firms/agribusi	Impacted owners
	c. Special Case: Legal monopoly (also see Sub2.1a, Sub2.3d)				
Sub2.3	**Controls/Bans on Business (Bans: Also see Sub2.6)**	All	Security/Safety		
⊙	a. Bans/Prohibition on business activities	All	Security/Safety	Illegal Operators/Traffick	Traffickees-victims
	b. Regulatory Oversight (of industry; also see Policy 6b)	National	Security/Safety	Competing firms	Victims, Consumers
	c. Directed Production/Operations (with private ownership)	All	Fairness/Morality	Exempt firms*, officials	Producers, Consumers
	d. Legal Monopoly: Adjudicators/localities (also Sub2.2c, Sub2.5c)	All	Security, Fairness	Offenders (wealthy/connecte	Victims, plaintiffs
Sub2.4	**Labor Interventions /incl. via Central Planning**				
⊙	a. wage controls: caps; conscription/involuntary servitude		Growth/Security	Certain firms	Competing employers,
	b. wage controls: floors		Fairness/Morality	Competing firms	Job seekers
⊙	c. Labor In-migration restrictions/bans (also see Sub2.3a)		Security	Illegal operators, competing workers	Foreign labor
⊙	d. Forced relocations/collectivization/expulsions, including genocide/policy-aided famines; also see Sub 2. 2a and b)		Fairness/Morality or Security	Users of labor	ictims; property owne
Sub2.5	**Property, Cost and Income Interventions**	All	Growth	Property acquirers	
	a. Land Rezoning (Land reforms see Sub2.2a)				Prior owners
⊙	b. Cost Transfers: Contaminated property, business costs			Offenders, favored firms	Cleanup costs; taxpayers
⊙	c. Judicial immunity by policy (including tacit policy; see Sub2.3d)			Offenders	Victims
	d. Fines/ Penalties/ Compensatory Damages				
	e. Legal purchasing requirements	All	Security	Firms, Sys2 staffing	Affected consumers
	f. Public-private partnerships (with financial immunity)	All	Growth/stability	Favored firms	ompeting firms, taxpayer
Sub2.6	**Product Restrictions/Bans; Tariffs; Sanctions**	National	Security	Officials/black marketeer	Consumers, some firm
⊙	a. Food Supply/Distribution (Food as Weapon)	National	Security	Competing firms	Victims/consumers
	b. Regulatory Non-Approval	National	Security (Safety)	New Admin unit, firms	tients seeking treatme
	c. Concessions in Exchange for Sovereignty (Free trade, fiscal/tax)	Nat'l, Supra	Growth		Payers, local decisions

SUBSYSTEM 2 of System 2

II. FIAT LAW OTHER OVERRIDING --Cont'd

SUBSYSTEM 2 PHASES: Hypothesized elevated risk of occurrence (including delayed impacts)

Sub2.#	A. POLICY INTERVENTION TYPE	Phase 1 (Initial)						Delay 1-Overshoot	Delay 2-Reversal		
		F. Rent-seeking activity	G. Impaired Production/Reduced Income Impacts	H. Shortages (incl. Food crises)	I. Black markets/violence due to contract non-legality	J. Clustering: Oversupply/ excess. Spec. and competition		K. Deficit/Debt (Expend.-> Inflows)	L. Secondary Policies / Impacts (incl. extra-judicial/ state violence)	M. Ownership insecurity (incl. self); hoarding	N. Visible protests/ unrest
Sub2.1	**Price Controls**										
0	a. Price or Quantity controls (caps)	1	1	*P fixed low	1	*P fixed high		1	Deregulation	1	
	b. Foreign exchange rates/currency controls (see Sub3.5b)		varies	*P = price					Rationing; supply		After removal
	c. Special Case: Control of Information (perception management)	1									
Sub2.2	**Prop. Ownership Interventions/Central Planning [See Sub2.4d]**										
0	a. Expropriations/seizures/transfers; land reforms	1	1	1	1			1	Liberalization	1	1
0	b. Private property bans; forced communal ownership		1	1	1			1	Crackdowns	1	1
	c. Special Case: Legal monopoly (also see Sub2.1a, Sub2.3d)								Asset Sales		
Sub2.3	**Controls/Bans on Business (Bans: Also see Sub2.6)**								Budget cuts; out-migration		
0	a. Bans/Prohibition on business activities	1	1	1	1			1	Crackdowns	1	
	b. Regulatory Oversight (of industry, also see Policy 6b)	1	1	1	1	1				1	
	c. Directed Production/Operations (with private ownership)	1	1	1*		1			Crackdowns	1	1
	d. Legal Monopoly: Adjudicators/localities (also Sub2.2c, Sub2.5c)	1	1					1			
Sub2.4	**Labor Interventions /incl. via Central Planning**		*of unbiased adjudication						Deregulation		
0	a. wage controls: caps; conscription/involuntary servitude	1	1	1*	1			1		1	1
	b. wage controls: floors	1	1	*of labor elsewhere		1b		1	Social welfare+	1	After removal
0	c. Labor in-migration restrictions/bans (also see Sub2.3a)	1	1	1	1a			1	Crackdowns	1	
0	d. Forced relocations/collectivization/expulsions, including genocide/policy-aided famines; also see Sub 2. 2a and b)	1	1	1				1	Crackdowns	1	1
				1a. Human trafficking		1b increased supply of job seekers					
Sub2.5	**Property, Cost and Income Interventions**										
0	a. Land Rezoning (Land reforms see Sub2.2a)	1							Compensation	1	
0	b. Cost Transfers: Contaminated property, business costs	1							Prosecution	1	
0	c. Judicial immunity by policy (including tacit policy; see Sub2.3d)	1							Prosecution	1	Families, Victims
	d. Fines/ Penalties/Compensatory Damages	1	1						Judicial system	1	
	e. Legal purchasing requirements	1	1						Enforcement Actions	1	
	f. Public-private partnerships (with financial immunity)	1						1	Sale; liquidation	1	
Sub2.6	**Product Restrictions/Bans; Tariffs; Sanctions**										
0	a. Food Supply/Distribution (Food as Weapon)	1	1	1	1			1	Crackdowns	1	1
	b. Regulatory Non-Approval	1	1	1	1			1	Crackdowns	1	1
	c. Concessions in Exchange for Sovereignty (Free trade, tax harmonization)								Crackdowns		

Sub2. 1. Price Controls

Manipulation of prices is often justified based on fairness goals but can produce unexpected and counterintuitive results that may connect to other policy actions and secondary policies. Major unintended outcomes of controlled pricing are *shortages, waste,* and *losses* for producers. *Policy-induced distortions in pricing* as a cause of shortages is generally acknowledged, but the role of price controls leading to oversupply and *waste* is less-known. Price controls often are imposed in conjunction with *subsidies* to firms, as detailed in **Sub1.4a**. For further understanding of prices, cost, and loss, see Appendix 1.

Sub2.1a. Price or Quantity controls/caps

Price Controls: Food and Necessities. A particularly dangerous policy involves controlling the price of a good at a price near or below the ability of the businesses to cover their production costs; historically such policies often affect *farmers**).

Costs and Change. The common error in policies attempting to set arbitrary "fair" prices is reference to some estimated fixed *cost of production* of the given product. Because *costs* and *consumer demand* change constantly, knowledge of what the price *should* be is impossible; *market participants* who daily suffer the consequences of instantaneous changes in demand, costs and prices also have imperfect knowledge but their continued survival depends upon acting upon the information (Re: Skin in the game; Taleb 2016b). Regarding the concept of "just price" refer to de La Calle (1544), and *imperfect knowledge*, Hayek (1945, 1974).

Loss, Production, and Shortages. Pricing policy that sets an arbitrary fixed price puts producers in the precarious position of potentially sustaining losses as things change. If they continue to produce at the controlled price, losses, bankruptcy, and destitution can result. In the face of price controls, struggling producers/farmers may cause goods to be in short and inconsistent supply, leading to long lines (queues) for consumers, especially for necessities.

Price controls on one type of crop can encourage a shift of production towards production of other crops. A case in point is a historical shift in land-use patterns away from *food crops* towards the more policy- incentivized *export/cash-crops*, leading to reduced food supply for the local population. (Brown in Schulz (Ed.) 1978:90, Lofchie 1978a: 563).

Impacts on Productivity. When faced with controlled prices, farmers have been *less likely* to use yield-increasing fertilizers, a policy-induced barrier to increased food production. (GAO 1975)

Food Crises. In extreme cases, price controls can result in the complete *cessation of production* when prices are set lower than the cost of production; in agricultural markets, this can lead to food supply disruptions, hunger, and famine. (General Accounting Office (GAO), 1975: 8; Kamuanga as cited in Eicher 1982; Coyne and Coyne 2015).

Additional Notes

To gain political support from urban populations, officials who seek election or re-election among their urban-based constituents have instituted price controls on certain agricultural goods to lower prices for their constituents who are largely urban consumers.

Price controls also can be instituted through *state marketing* or *grain boards* that purchase agricultural produce for export at a pre-determined government price. (Eicher 1982)

Price controls in conjunction with overvalued currencies (See **Sub3.5b**) can severely reduce the incomes of farmers.

Rental Markets. Note that regarding *real estate rentals* (most notably rentals in apartment buildings within metropolitan areas), price controls as a policy intervention can be referred to as *rent control*, in which some form of legal limits/caps are placed on increases in rents. Longer-term, there is a risk of shortages of housing as developers/builders may have a disincentive to add supply due to lower projected returns. Although initially renters may appear to benefit from the policy, benefits long-term may be unclear without knowing what rents would be had additional housing been supplied in the absence of price controls; if housing shortages develop under such a policy, it is likely that landlords will be induced to progressively raise rents to the legal limit.

Property Abandonment, Crime, and Urban Blight. Similar to farmers who cease production under price controls, owners of real estate faced with mounting costs, liability, rent controls and regulatory difficulties may opt to abandon the properties. When enough properties are affected, entire neighborhoods and zones can become essentially ownerless; fewer people may be present to help maintain the safety and security of the area. This creates opportunities for others to occupy the properties, which in combination with less security can lead to increased danger for both outsiders and the occupants. Criminal activity in blighted areas may also be linked to activities or products banned by policy (See **Sub2.3a** and **Sub2.6**).

Interventions can also involve local officials preventing real estate transactions from taking place at agreed-upon prices between buyer and seller. See **Sub2.3c** regarding controls that are *not* related to real estate transaction prices, rents, and rental income, but rather, official overrides of real estate operation management and property owner decision-making.

Controls on the Quantities of Goods Produced. Dictated quantities of goods to be produced is more likely to be a feature of *central planning* where a functional pricing system doesn't exist other than what bureaucrats decide (Mises 1920). Also see **Sub2.2a** and **Sub2.2b** related to central planning tendencies. Such quantity dictates/quotas may also exist in wartime.

Controls on quantities may tend to be in conjunction with some form of price control (dictated or fixed price), discussed above.

When some semblance of a market does exist and producers must absorb the costs of their dictated production quota, an inappropriate quota may cause interruptions in supply if producers sustain *losses* associated with required production amount. If losses are occurring, it is also likely that to continue in operation, the targeted businesses would have a strong incentive to avail themselves of alternative supply or distribution routes, leading to the possible development of black markets and subsequent crackdowns when quota violations have been discovered.

Shortages may emerge in pockets as certain supplies of the goods disappear and reappear in and out of dictated supply and black-market channels (See **Col I** for further discussion of black markets).

Deregulation: After Removal of Controls. When price controls are removed in a reversal phase deregulation move, the prices may adjust markedly *upward* to reflect actual costs and demand. This could cause consumer backlash and protests as many are not accustomed to the higher prices; however, goods may be more plentiful than before, reducing the need to wait in long lines.

During the transition from regulated (price controls) to unregulated, some entrepreneurs with *advance knowledge* of the change may move to hoard supplies to take advantage of the upcoming deregulation; while those doing this are understandably vilified for this, *previously unsustainable* policy interventions in pricing are likely at the root of the problem.

For further detail and illustrations of pricing and costs, see Appendix 1.

Sub2.1c. Special Case: Control of Information (perception management)

In previous discussions on distortions of human behavior, and price distortions, *perception management* was identified as a possible source of behavioral and price distortions. This category is limited to the case of *official* control of the information, including by media/news outlets that might be disseminating the "official story" under the guise of presenting the facts. As noted, such a System 2 distortion may tend to remain in place indefinitely as long as the policy can be enforced, or until there is disruption (e.g. shortages) that induces a policy change. Disinformation is believed to be a feature of both System 1 and 2. Important differences may arise due to the level of *centralization* or *decentralization* of information, and central planning (**Sub2.2**).

Case Study. Consider a situation in which news is accurately disseminated of an outbreak of tainted meat (e.g. infected with salmonella). This information causes panic and meat purchases in the region or country as well as prices plummet and stores stop stocking product until the problem is resolved.

Information Suppression #1. In official news reports, health officials wish to calm the public by stating that normality has been restored and that the situation is under control. Assume that the problem had *not* really been contained despite their assurances. Panic subsides, public confidence is restored, prices rise and meat consumption resumes leading to *more cases* of food poisoning. While this *is* official disinformation, some might argue that the intent of the public officials to maintain calm and order was reasonable.

Information Suppression #2. Public officials embarrassed by continued outbreaks following their public pronouncements, attempt to suppress all information concerning the outbreaks. The oblivious public continues to consume tainted meat and food poisoning continues. Prices remain stable when they should reflect reduced consumption due to the dangers.

Some takeaways from this example are: (a) **Economic distortions**. *Flawed* information suggests that prices may have existed for products that should have been removed from the shelves; as for products that are deemed safe and being offered in stores, instead of their prices being unusually depressed reflecting something amiss in the overall market, prices seemed to reflect normal conditions. (b) **Centralization of information** is considered particularly dangerous since alternative, competing sources of information are not available to protect citizens when officials decide on suppression. (c) **Accountability and Cost-Bearing**. In addition to the loss of public trust, the question remains whether public officials who gain from taxpayer funds, but whose actions led public harm, should be held accountable and bear the associated costs (compensation for damages, etc.; also Re: Skin in the Game, Taleb 2016b).

Sub2. 2. Property Ownership Interventions/Central Planning
Sub2.2a. Expropriations/seizures/transfers; land reforms

Wealth Transfer. Expropriations and seizures of property can involve substantial transfers of wealth from one party to another even though the actions may enjoy popular support for (social) justice or even law-and-order objectives. Incumbent political leaderships can gain by taking control of private or public (government-owned) property over a period of years. Expropriations and property seizures may also arise in an overthrow of the existing order in a coup d'état, or "revolution," etc. by a "new" leadership. (Also see **Column N,** protest/unrest)

While expropriations and seizures of private property may satisfy a desire for justice to be served, the facts may not justify the policy and the solution may cause intended or unintended consequences.

Expropriation and Land Redistribution/Reforms. It is generally agreed that *return of stolen property* to the original owners/victims is part of the enforcement of property rights. In countries that have a large landowning class that is the beneficiary of previous land-transfer policies through political connections, policies may be proposed to return the tracts to the rightful owners (e.g. expropriated peasants/farmers).

Policy vs. Judiciary. A question is why the injustice could not be resolved through the judicial system whereby after a ruling in favor of the victims, the land is legally transferred back to the rightful owners (or equivalent compensation is given). Purported injustices must be examined on a case-by-case basis; it should be noted that policy interventions under the guise of "reforms" might have other motives which are not always obvious and which may not lead to justice being served, or which may intentionally or unintentionally benefit some at the expense of others.

One concern with land reform as a *policy* rather than as a *judicial means* of redress, is the role of politically-connected local or foreign agribusinesses; these entities may have a strong incentive to support policies that reduce competition for their goods as well as to maintain higher prices through policy-controlled supply/production. For example, *legislated restrictions on farm size* can prevent farms from operating economically since farm technology and investments in land improvement may require larger landholdings to be economic (Hopper in Schulz 1978). Another policy is *forced communal ownership* of redistributed lands which tend to reduce the capacity to produce greater quantities of foods and in some cases, have led to famine. Communal ownership is further discussed in **Sub2.2b**.

Land Quality. Another concern is the land itself: Do the peasants receive the *same* land that was taken from them or are they given vaguely-defined "equivalent" parcels? If substitute parcels are given, is the quality capable of reaching the previous level of food production? In some cases, land transfers might involve marginal low-yield, labor-intensive tracts. Another question is how the policy compensates the landowners whose land was expropriated in the reform for their loss. Did the land reform allow them to shed marginal quality property to be compensated with better quality parcels (or other types of compensation) elsewhere?

Civil Asset Forfeiture. It is also possible for property to be seized when the property is suspected to have been purchased with proceeds of illegal transactions. Such seizures can constitute a sizable source of supplementary income for investigating units.

Nationalizations. A highly appealing popular argument for nationalizing a business/ industry is that the industry's wealth can be the source of *social welfare* benefits for the citizenry. However, it is unlikely that the expropriation will be accompanied by a concomitant policy to reduce *income-based fees (e.g. income and other taxes)*; System 2 derivative inflows thereafter consist of *two* sources:

1. *Revenues* of the expropriated business*; and

2. Income-based fees (taxes). Should the business begin to fail, taxes can be relied upon to cover the losses. Once this dynamic is in place, the nationalized business is likely to eventually reflect the reinforcing feedback loop of System 2, which means disincentives to control costs--derivative inflows rather than *revenues less costs* (e.g. profit-and-loss accounting) become the fallback.

Ownership Transfers. With nationalizations (private business expropriations), the stock ownership can be transferred to the new leadership and/or cronies via various means, then paying themselves or relatives salaries, bonuses, and funneling funds through contracts to relatives and their closer supporters (inner circle); all depends on the arrangements they make.

In a later phase leading to the overshoot, the nationalized entity may be facing financial distress and bankruptcy, requiring *more* taxpayer funds to keep the entity in operation.

Post-Overshoot Liberalization. Following the overshoot in a reversal phase of the feedback loop, a policy of liberalization may be adopted to reform the economy; privatizations and public offerings can result in the proceeds of the stock sales going to public officials and their supporters who may have seized a portion of ownership during the nationalization process.

Legal Monopoly or State Control. In the discussion on price controls (**Sub2.1** above), policy may expand to take over the ownership and/or control of an industry while *legally* forbidding competition (*Legal* is contrasted with *natural* monopoly). A legal (i.e. by law) monopoly may be justified as in the public interest and to provide lower prices or better-quality services to the poor.

However, even under public control the challenges of pricing and supply remain. Losses are no less a threat to state-owned enterprises and legal monopolies. However, there is a possible back-up source of funds in System 2 --income-based inflows (i.e. taxpayer funds) that-- if legally permitted--can be drawn upon to subsidize any losses of these types of enterprises; these funds can be provided either as loans or as direct subsidies. Contradictorily, when state enterprises are subsidized with tax funds, efforts to alleviate poverty may in part be paid for by the taxpaying poor themselves (minus administrative costs).

Legal monopoly is also linked to category **Sub2.3d** with a focus on two areas that have something resembling legal monopolies: *Adjudication services* and *jurisdictional localities* (e.g. municipalities).

Sub2.2b. Restrictions/ban on private property; forced communal ownership

Central Planning. The acquisition of private property by the state (e.g. the former Soviet Union) may tend to be associated with a far-reaching policy intervention called *central planning*. Broadly stated, central administrative unit(s) generally both own and control the production and distribution system of all or part of an economy. This is also related to certain *labor interventions--* **Sub2.4d forced relocations/collectivization**.

The critical problems inherent in central planning have been addressed by many observers since shortly after the Russian revolution (Mises, *Economic Calculation in the Socialist Commonwealth* 1920; Hayek 1944; Lévy 1977; Voslensky 1984; Reisman 2014] and evidenced by the dissolution of the Soviet Union in December 1991.

Because central planning involves a large transfer of power to System 2 entities (national or central governments) there is believed to be a very elevated risk of not only abuse of power on a larger scale, but also misallocation of resources in such a way that food shortages and famine may be more likely. The record of centrally-planned states in terms of lives lost (including genocide and mass starvations by policy) during the 20th century have also been documented (Re: Rummel 1997; Re: *democide*).

Note: It should be clarified that **Sub2.2b** most closely corresponds to *socialism* in its *original meaning* (Marx 1867): *State ownership of the means of production*. Modern states and parties that describe themselves as *communist* might be more closely aligned with the original meaning of socialism, but this may vary. Modern states and parties that describe themselves as *socialist* can generally be thought of as highly *redistributive* (heavy emphasis on initial high-percentage decoupling and expansion of **Sub1** policy interventions).

A form of central planning in the monetary realm exists in **Subsystem 3** but with different outcomes.

Communal Landholding. This policy also relates to *labor interventions* (e.g. forced relocations/villageization) in **Sub2.4d** below. There, examples of collective agriculture and communal landholding policies (Re: Ujamaa policy, Tanzania) are noted as well as the subsequent food crises of 1972-1974. Policies instituting *cooperative societies* where long-term private ownership of land is prohibited may lead to disincentives for the members to invest in long-term land improvement (Hopper in Shultz 1978: 76)

Drought is often used as a catch-all explanation for food shortages and crises, yet communal land ownership can be the fundamental cause which droughts (often common to the affected areas) only exacerbated. Communal ownership of land in the food crises of 1968-1973 in the Sahelian region of Africa may have played a critical role (Economist 1983:76).

Centralized Food Procurement and Distribution. Policies to redistribute food to the poor through a form of central planning in agriculture may initially appear to be praiseworthy. However, the intervention in the food distribution process and related policies (such as zonal or interstate restrictions, price controls, subsidization) can lead to significant misallocation of food supplies. In extreme examples, it has been documented that while international relief is being sought for famine-struck areas, other areas of the country maintain surplus stocks of food grain (Schuh in Schultz 1978: 309; General Accounting Office 1975: 55). Also see **Sub2.6a** regarding food supply/distribution blockages.

Sub2.2c Legal Monopoly

See **Sub2.1a Revenue Controls** and **Sub2.3d. Competing Adjudicators/Municipalities;** in the monetary realm, see **Sub3.3.**

Sub2.3. Controls/Bans on Business Activity

Sub2.3a. Regulatory Bans on Business Activity. This type of policy intervention focuses on certain (typically illegal or highly suspect) businesses (for interventions targeting *labor* or specific *goods/products*, see **Sub2.4** and **Sub2.6**, respectively). In this intervention as well as **Sub2.4** and **Sub2.6**, violence and human rights abuses can result due to the absence of legally-enforceable contracts (for labor, distribution rights, etc.).

Human Trafficking. The international problem of *human trafficking* (e.g. black markets in workers/) may have some of its roots in policy interventions that ban certain activities for which there is a demand. One widespread example is *prostitution*. In some countries prostitution is legal, but subject to heavy regulatory guidelines. Where the practice is banned, black markets are likely to develop.

Because by definition, the activity is illegal, the *safety of the victims* cannot be monitored or assured; *the laws unintentionally facilitate a transfer of power from victim to abuser*. Should a victim complain of abuse, the illegality of the activity renders them powerless to seek legal action against the perpetrators. For this reason, laws have in some cases been modified as a compromise, to *legalize* the activity for one group (e.g. the seller of the services) and conditionally *illegal* for the other (the buyer of the services), Should the seller be mistreated they can in theory legally file charges against the buyer. Outright decriminalization has been pursued or recommended in other cases and countries (Human Rights Council 2013; Reisenwitz 2014).

Sub2.3b. Regulatory Oversight of Industry. This intervention is also related to the regulation of some pharmaceutical products in **Sub2.6b**). By law, many industries and business activities are subject to regulatory bodies (aka regulators) and requirements such as *occupational licensing* for certain businesses (e.g. hairstylists). While regulation appears to be reasonably designed to improve consumer safety, it is easy to overlook potential distortions—some even leading to potential fatalities.

Rent-seeking gives competing businesses an incentive to use the regulatory body to *restrict competition* and/or provide *new business opportunities* for themselves. This serves as a policy-aided tool to raise returns for these businesses at the expense of would-be competitors and start-ups, as well as individuals wishing to work in the fields; the laws require them to undergo potentially time-consuming and expensive *occupational licensing* requirements that keeps them off the market as competitors to existing establishments (Also see **Sub2.5e**).

Regulations may be in part drafted or proposed by the *very industries* being regulated, giving themselves a certain self-serving set of rules to "abide" by, protecting themselves from liability--in essence, insulating themselves from full accountability (Re: policy-aided cost avoidance).

The regulators are under intense pressure and must be careful of their own reputations; a misstep subject to public scrutiny can potentially destroy the career of a regulatory bureaucrat. Therefore, there is likely to be an inherent bias towards decision by committee to share the responsibility, as well as a certain level of *inaction* or at least delay. This can result in an *inherent incapacity to respond to changing conditions and technologies in a timely manner*. Problems that surface within the industry or a firm may be acknowledged but the pace of corrective action may be particularly slow; in some sense, the more *serious* the problem, the more the incentive to temporize (procrastinate). When action is taken, it may take forms that leave open the probability of reoccurrence in the future. In the event of an industrial accident or crisis, regulators will be incented to take action with "tougher regulations" or perhaps a token firing of either a perceived out-of-line official or senior manager of the firm to appease the public that the problem has been corrected; however, regulatory oversight gives the regulated some *protection against liability claims in court as long as they can point to having kept in conformity with the established regulatory guidelines* at the time of the accident. (Also see *judicial immunity* **Sub2.5c**)

Another scenario also can involve banning of products by a regulatory agency (See **Sub2.6** related to product bans and prohibition.

Sub2.3c. Directed Production/Operations (private ownership)
Here, private ownership of a business or property/ real estate is permitted, but the authorities may dictate what is to be produced and possibly the quantities to be produced. The operations of the business may also be under strict controls in which the decisions of business owners or managers may be overridden for a variety of functions including purchasing, expenditures, labor, etc. As a matter of *national policy,* this type of intervention might be traditionally referred to as *fascism*, although individual policy interventions of this nature can occur at various administrative levels. Both producers and consumers can be adversely affected (Col E) because absent the intervention different products and quantities might have been produced that *responded better to*

consumer needs and provided greater returns to producers. At the national level, the action may primarily be justified for national security priorities, fairness, or growth; at more local levels, the justifications may also be growth and development and fairness (labor and anti-discrimination laws, apartment renter rights, etc.). With regard to *real estate*, this category covers policy intervention that control operations and property owner decision-making. Controls on rents and transaction prices (i.e. *rent control*) applies to **Sub2.1a**.

Sub2.3d. Legal Monopolies in Adjudication and Localities (Sub2.2c Legal Monopolies covered here and partly in **Sub2.1a).**

Certain public services are assumed to be provided by legal monopoly. From the standpoint of economic distortions, the fundamental issue concerns whether under such an institutional arrangement, offenders can be expected to incur the *full costs* of their actions. If not, the problem of *moral hazard* and persecution with impunity (**Sub2.5c Judicial Immunity**) remain, and (social) injustices are believed likely to persist. Two areas addressed here are *adjudication* and *localities*.

Legal Monopolies: Justice System. This topic is closely related to **Sub2.5c** (Judicial Immunity) in which judicial bias exists and/or the authorities fail to prosecute. The court system is a crucial element in establishing *safeguards* that can improve the prospects for justice. However, it is possible for *extra-judicial* actions, *fiat law* and political sanctions to be resorted to instead of the courts, resulting in additional injustices and capricious abuses of power by authorities.

The process of establishing immunity can begin at the lawmaking stage: If legislation can be determined by "politicking" there is still ample means for a wealthy and politically-connected dishonest individuals (whether in business or politics) to *bypass or override* the judicial system* by rent-seeking and lobbying politicians/public officials for *fiat laws* that grant impunity, special privileges, or exemptions/loopholes. (Re: rent-seeking, lobbying, bribes).

Overriding authority through policy means is the central nature of **Subsystem 2** of System 2.

Judicial Bias. While it can be argued that reliance on the judicial system can be a preferable alternative to fiat law overrides as described briefly above, a major unresolved matter concerns the risk that powerful, wealthy, and/or politically-connected offenders and/or their supporters might use the court system to sway decisions in their favor or to push for *non-prosecution* (e.g. bribing the judges, etc.)

Adjudication and a Market for Neutrality. If the current judicial system is essentially a judicial *monopoly* without a mechanism to allow for *competition in neutrality (neutral adjudication), the risk of injustice remains high.* A System 2 monopoly in the provision of justice may restrict the development of a market in *neutral adjudication*, to be detailed below. A proximate solution is the ability for a market in *adjudication services* to develop such that judicial organizations/firms (employing judges and attorneys) can compete on their ability to render judgement in a *neutral* manner (Re: neutral adjudication).

It should be noted that to some extent such solutions exist already in the form of *settling out of court* or *binding arbitration*, an alternative to seeking justice through the court system. However, it appears that generally current legal systems do not permit the outright establishment of *private judges/adjudication services* that would compete with the existing court adjudication system (this restriction is categorized in **Sub2.3d** and **Sub 2.2c** *legal monopoly* may also apply).

Just as attorneys and other professionals in various fields including Certified Public Accountants can be ranked according to various criteria, formal adjudication services can also be ranked according to their reputation for *neutrality*. Moreover, since there would likely be various court locations available to plaintiffs rather than a single court location, the problem of *clogged courts* and slow processing of court cases may also be diminished.

The *affordability* of adjudication services remains a concern. Just as personal injury attorneys are hired to help people seek compensation (in accidents, etc.) adjudication services might be hired in a similar way, or in conjunction with the attorney selected. But the legitimate question arises whether the victim can afford the services. If the market becomes more *competitive* (as could be argued may be the case in the market for *personal injury lawyers*) it is possible that the *cost of services* might be reduced over time--or as is currently the case, the client pays little or nothing and both the client and attorney split some percentage of the proceeds of a lawsuit.

[For additional references on law and alternative legal systems see Bastiat 1850; Leoni 1961; Rothbard, 1981; Friedman 2001; Benson 2011; Re: Tort law; Ralph Nader; compensation for damages, etc.] On the *rule of law* and cases: Aristotle (c. 350 B.C.), Locke (1689), Madison (1788), Mitchell (2014), Hanke (2015), Parkinson (2017)].

Legal Monopolies: Localities. Typically, the residents of localities such as municipalities have no opt-out clause or ability to change municipal providers if they so choose. It is also possible for property or other forms of income or value-based taxes to rise at rates higher than consumer prices. This is likely attributable to the legal monopoly status that these entities enjoy over the residents within their jurisdictions. The reinforcing feedback loop can lead to an eventual outmigration of residents to lower-tax cities and regions of the country. This contributes to lower revenues for the city (and/or county) causing financial pressures. Localities that reach the overshoot point may attempt budget cutbacks or renegotiate their debt repayment with creditors.

The liberalization of laws allowing competition in the space for local area management and planned communities could give property owners the option of selecting service plans at fixed monthly rates with *opt-out clauses* after an initial contract period, roughly like internet or phone providers. This could contribute to cost reductions in the provision of these services over time as these entities attempt to economize.

Sub2.4. Labor Interventions

Sub2.4a. Wage controls: Caps, Conscription, and Involuntary Servitude.

Wage caps can exist in various forms. In periods of high inflation, wartime, or other national emergencies the argument for capping wages may be accepted by the public for certain industries, including for service in the armed forces. A notable case involving legally fixed wages and wage caps involves *conscription*, including required service either in the military (aka *the draft*) or the court system (e.g. jury duty).

Col D: The conscription can produce beneficiaries including larger budgets for the related government departments, as well as private firms that may also make use of the conscripted labor either directly or indirectly.

Col H: Shortages of labor can arise when individuals are conscripted and pulled out of the private labor force.

Col N: Anti-war movements (e.g. anti-draft protests, card-burnings) can result from conscription policies for military service.

War and Conflict. Although not specifically provided for in a column category is the critical issue of war. Involuntarily conscripted personnel sent into battle or conflict zones--predominantly young people--have historically been victims. This includes in some areas the involuntary recruitment of child soldiers. Although it might be argued that war and the risk of violent conflicts might be on the decline in modern times, accounting for *tail risk* can lead to more sobering conclusions (Pinker 2012; Cirillo and Taleb 2015; for complexity analysis of conflicts see Fellman, et al. 2016).

It is recognized that *some* individuals may not be opposed to being conscripted in the sense that they would have been content to accept similar employment at a similar wage for a similar time period with a similar level of danger (Re: dangerous jobs).

Human Rights Issues. This is not necessarily an argument against *voluntary* military or security services, national security needs, or court-administered justice. It is the *involuntary* servitude to these ends that creates distortions with *human rights* implications (Re: *Universal declaration of human rights*).

Cost-Return Decoupling. The issue of legal conscription and involuntary servitude highlights *human rights violations* with clarity because in the extreme, one must bear the *entire cost* of one's labor while receiving none of the returns associated with the cost: i.e. nothing in exchange (other than perhaps just enough food to continue laboring).

Human Rights: Financial and Economic Aspects. The cost-return coupling bond concept suggests that human rights and *economy* go together—*both* are expected to be adversely affected by human rights violations. Digging deeper one might ask: Can human rights violations be somehow *positively* related to economic growth? Isn't it entirely possible for a firm to financially benefit by forcefully conscripting (enslaving) individuals to use their involuntary labor? While it is true that a firm could potentially benefit *financially*, by its *involuntary nature*, such an activity no longer *economic* (Walker 1888). The confusion lies in conflating *financial* and *economic* while ignoring the cost-return coupling bond concept: In the involuntary servitude scenario, the laborer bears the cost while the firm reaps the benefit – financially beneficial to the firm but an economic distortion where returns are decoupled from associated costs.

While many might agree that involuntary servitude is unacceptable, it could easily be pointed out that many of us work for a living at wages which may at best just cover the cost of living (Re: Living wage). In this sense, people may feel that their situation is involuntary in that they feel trapped and unable to escape; in addition, the problem of declining *real* wages from inflation is detailed in Subsystem 3.

Putting aside the options of self-employment, entrepreneurship, or building greater marketable skills that might command higher wages, this serious and real concern-- being paid too little for one's labor--gives rise to calls for policy interventions imposing a floor on wages. This is addressed in the next section, **Sub2.4b**.

Although sometimes overlooked, human rights violations can extend beyond labor; individuals acting in various roles, whether as workers, managers, business owners, merchants (buyers bidding or sellers offering) can all be subject to some form of policy intervention that infringes upon and overrides their ability to decide by and for themselves; on this topic, see individualism vs. collectivism; Appendix 2).

Sub2.4b. Wage Controls: Floors

Although not immediately recognized, potential beneficiaries of wage floors (i.e. minimum wages) include *manufacturers* of automated equipment/robotics to replace more expensive labor establishments, *high-end restaurants* that already pay higher wages to their employees and are thereby unaffected by the higher minimum wage (these restaurants may gain some customers from restaurants closing down or moving away due to the higher costs), *neighboring restaurants just outside of the jurisdiction* where the law takes effect may see increased customer traffic after restaurants within the jurisdiction close down due to higher legislated minimum wage costs.

The debate over the effects of minimum wages is complicated by the presence of *nominal* vs. *real* wages. In a price-inflationary environment, businesses may be able to absorb higher nominal wage costs because their *nominal revenues* are rising as well. Clever politicians may be able to time the policies to coincide with inflation so that the policy's adverse impacts are not felt as greatly. Therefore, studies that do not account for changes in nominal and real wages (adjusting for inflation) may be misleading as to the impacts of wage floors.

Some policymakers recognizing the need for wage flexibility and responsiveness to job-seeker and employer needs have instituted legal compromises such as minimum wage *tier systems* (varying wage rates) based on certain criteria.

Sub2.4c. Labor In-migration restrictions

What is often called *illegal* immigration is closely related to **Sub2.3a. Regulatory Bans on Business Activity.** The international problem of *human trafficking* (*black markets for illegal workers*) may have some of its roots in policy interventions that ban entry for labor in countries in which there is a demand.

Because it is illegal to enter and work in the country without proper authorization, the undocumented migrants/laborers tend to be kept underground. Similar to **Sub2.3a**, because by definition they are illegal, the *safety of the laborers* cannot be monitored or assured, and abuse is more likely to be unpunished because the laborers have no legal recourse. The absence of a legal framework for international labor facilitates a transfer of power to (potential) abusers and human rights injustices may be more likely to result. It should be pointed out that undocumented workers are likely to be victimized at least *four* times: First, in the process of *human trafficking* itself including scams, mistreatment by the traffickers, deaths of concealed migrants in transit; second, by employers who benefit from the lowered costs of abusing their illegal employees because of the illegality of the labor; third, by illegal or legal co-workers or associates who may make attempts at extortion by threatening to "turn them in" if they don't do something for them; fourth, in a crackdown **(Col L)** by the authorities, they can also suffer abuse in detention and deportation. This multiple victimization pattern also is likely in **Sub2.3a**.

Sub2.4d Forced Relocations/Collectivization/Expulsions

Labor interventions can also be linked to property expropriations. In the case of forced relocations, collectivization and expulsions, property owners may lose their homes and businesses in various ways. One is official expropriation and transfer to other parties, with the proceeds going to the System 2 administrative unit(s). This type of policy is seen as particularly dangerous due to the higher risk of genocide.

Rhetorical justifications for such policies vary, but *fairness* (including *equality and social justice*) is an important and popular justification which might mask other objectives, noted below.

Historical record. Programs ostensibly to promote a philosophy of more *moral production methods* can involve communal ownership. The immorality of private ownership and capitalist methods can also be used as a justification for the *relocation* of vast numbers of laborers and resettlement into collectivized agricultural camps and/or production units.

Collective agriculture and communal landholding policies such as *Ujamaa* (Tanzania) have a tragic history. Prior to the policy the nation was a leading food producer (Rake, 1975); the 1972-1974 food crisis ensued following these policy interventions. Moreover, brutal crackdowns ensued when villagers resisted. (Lofchie 1978b). Also see **Sub2 and Sub2.2b** (including Central Planning).

As explained elsewhere in the subject of *fascism* which includes *national socialism*; *Nazism*), the rhetorical justification for *fairness* combined with the singling out of a minority *deemed as wealthy and/or evil* can lead to policies of relocation and genocide (Re: Jews and the Holocaust; also refer to the history and origins of the targeting of Tutsi in the 1994 Rwandan genocide (Re: Hutu power).

In the U.S. during World War II, Japanese-Americans were targeted and relocated with the rhetorical justification of national security. However, often overlooked was a possible ulterior motive: A property grab on *mortgaged* real estate. Japanese-American owners of real estate on the U.S. West coast with mortgages on the properties were at risk of default (inability to continue making the payments) on those properties when they were relocated and interned. After loan default, many properties may have transferred ownership at fire-sale prices, increasing the wealth of the property acquirers with the loss borne by the former owners. (Re: Japanese-American internment: Franklin Roosevelt).

Ulterior Motives of Policy. It is not always clear to what degree certain policies and programs are in fact *cover for other motives*. The forced expulsion, rounding up and/or extermination of certain groups may be intended to transfer ownership of property or clear land for new owners including developers and the politically-connected.

Tragically, policies may be uncritically observed by outsiders or those reporting on the events who are unfamiliar with the underlying realities, or are ideologically favorable to the cause or religion being promoted.

Sub2.5a, Land rezoning can result in "windfall" profits by policy for a zoning change that was previously unknown to the marketplace, and arranged privately between officials and a *"politically* entrepreneurial" business operator. Note that land rezoning policies can potentially take many forms and may have close links to this category: Land reforms in **Sub2.2a** or possibly forced relocations in **Sub2.4d**.

For example, an area that is zoned strictly as a public park suddenly has the deed restriction removed after the sale so that acquirer of the property now can use the property for *commercial* purposes, increasing the value potentially by a sizable amount.

A variation of this might be for properties that are acquired by an administrative unit of System 2 at taxpayer expense at property prices *far above* what could have been sold for in undistorted real estate markets. Beneficiaries would be the selling property owners and the real estate agent who may have received a higher-than-normal commission for their services; this does not necessarily imply that the beneficiaries are co-conspirators; it is entirely possible that the property is simply sold at *inflated prices* due to a miscalculation or misunderstanding of market prices by System 2 administrators. The key issue is the problem of decoupling: The control of resources that System 2 administrative units can have *at little or no cost* to System 2, with the decoupled potential returns available to others who benefit.

Sub2.5b. Transfers of Contaminated Property. In the environmental realm, the decoupling policy may involve an offending business that has polluted the land it occupies (e.g. toxic waste) and that does not wish to pay for the cost of cleanup. To avoid the cost of its actions (see **Col D**), the business lobbies for immunity or makes a private arrangement with officials for some form of transfer or land swap to transfer the property to *public ownership*. Subsequently, the property may be cleaned up at taxpayer expense (**Col E**: income-based payers/taxpayers as cost-bearers), or left as an environmental hazard.

If this impunity and lack of accountability is not corrected by the authorities who oversee the public land, the likelihood of continued environmental damage and abuse increases (Re: *moral hazard*). Often overlooked is that private property must be accompanied by *accountability* such that the owner absorbs the *full cost* of their actions with regards to the property; collusion between owners and public officials either through policymaking or private deal-making can reduce accountability (and costs to the offenders).

Sub2.5c. Judicial Immunity by Policy (Including Tacit). This category refers to countless possible cases in the context of both business and public service, including harm to humans or the environment, dishonest business practices including selling defective or mislabeled products, or overworking employees. The victims and their families may sue for compensation, but the business has conspired with public officials to prevent the case from going to court, or if the case does make it to court, the judges are instructed to be lenient or find minimal compensatory damages. (Re: *karoshi* death by overwork court cases, Japan).

Persecution and Limited Recourse. In a human rights context, many ethnic, religious groups and individuals may suffer persecution and be victims of violence and rape but have little or no support from law enforcement or recourse to justice through the courts because the court system may be heavily biased in favor of the ruling party's ethnic or religious group or belief systems that make light of human rights violations. Some crimes such as rape may be treated as lower priority in which the victim is unjustly blamed for having "brought it upon themselves."

Non-prosecution of weak enforcement may also be "tacit" in the sense that there is no explicit law stating that offenders of a particular group can enjoy impunity, but law enforcement tends to shelve certain types of crime cases and courts may tend to avoid hearing certain cases. Officials may tend to ignore state-led violence or refuse to prosecute offenders from favored/privileged groups, with the outcome that the justice system tacitly condones the violence. This can lead to a long-term build-up of resentments as noted in the next section.

Even if there is a commitment towards justice against violent offenders, it is also possible that priority is given to policy-instituted crimes as noted **Sub2.6** such that law enforcement resources are diverted towards the apprehension and prosecution of suspects for those crimes first (e.g. illegal drugs and the drug war; alcohol Re: *prohibition*).

Critical Linkage to Future Conflict. Protests may erupt **(Col N)** when local communities feel that they have been wronged by the authorities (or those supported by the authorities), and for *non-prosecution* of violence against the perpetrators. A strong sense of injustice can develop that leads to future tendencies towards retaliation, including the formation of –or joining forces with-- existing rebel or insurgent groups.

International pressure (human rights organizations, other countries) may be applied towards eventual prosecution of offenders; this is classified in secondary policies **(Col L)** and may play a role in reducing future conflict.

This category is closely related to **Sub2.3d Legal Monopoly** (Re: Adjudicators).

Sub2.5e, Legal Purchasing Requirements. Some interventions require by law that individuals or businesses purchase a specified product, raising their costs *legally*. This can apply to a variety of products, some based in private sector activity for an ostensible public purpose such as safety. Some examples include required insurance to cover minimum liability for damages, minimum accident insurance, and health insurance coverage. Occupational licensing, *permitting* of various kinds, and legally-mandated schooling/training/internship requirements are also common. The additional costs in time and financial commitments can lead to disincentives towards gainful employment if transfer payments (e.g. welfare benefits) are available instead, resulting in longer periods of unemployment and lower incomes.

Decoupling Point. Another area of legal purchasing requirements pertains to excessive/*involuntary income-based charges* detailed in the *fundamental decoupling* process when System 2 services are perceived to exceed their (voluntary) value. As long as the income-based payers (taxpayers) continue to have taxable income, they are *obligated* to pay. The consequences of the feedback loop (lower income, higher dependency incentives) resulting in an overshoot are noted elsewhere.

Legal purchasing requirements allow Sys1 businesses (e.g. insurance companies) greater returns by a legal increase in their revenues; for details on the health insurance industry see the relevant section in **Sub1.1a**; other businesses (e.g. existing hair salons) can benefit by restricting the supply of possible future competing businesses through various stringent *market entry* requirements such as occupational licensing and training. Because the *public safety* goal is a seemingly reasonable justification for these policy interventions, such requirements may remain in force regardless of their effectiveness. System 2 entities and employees are also beneficiaries of legal purchasing requirements in the sense noted above; this inflow serves to transfer more wealth to these individuals than might have otherwise existed.

Sub2.5f. Public-private partnerships (with financial immunity). There are numerous possible variations of this type of arrangement whereby officials work with private firms to develop a project for the purposes of growth or *urban redevelopment*. Initially, amid the fanfare, public officials may be elected and receive support for promoting such projects as a path to development, but the consequences over the longer-term and the risks of highly distortive outcomes may often be forgotten because the process can unravel over years.

The decoupling of returns from associated costs occurs when *taxpayers* are called upon to pay (all or a portion) of the costs of the project while private firms [including *contractors* who build the structure(s)] receive the benefits of any positive returns; this can include (part or all) the proceeds of an eventual sale, possibly even at a *loss to be absorbed by the taxpayers*. Moreover, if the new public-private partnership business competes with other local businesses, a problem of *oversupply* may occur that causes competing businesses to suffer financially, lowering their net income and income-based revenues, leading to financial hardship for the locality as well.

Sub2.6. Product Restrictions/Bans; Tariffs; Sanctions

Restrictions on products/goods are listed here; the restrictive variations are numerous. Import *tariffs* (a form of import tax) raise the cost of imports for consumers and users of the imported inputs in the importing country. Tariffs on imports also penalize *foreign producers* and opportunities for development of poor nations by raising the cost of their products. For example, tariff percentages may vary according to the degree of value-added in the product so that raw material products might have a low or zero tariff percentage while high-margin processed/manufactured goods have much higher tariffs. The impact on developing countries can be devastating: The economic distortions that result from such high-tariff regimes mean that development of higher-margin processed/ manufactured goods industries --an important factor for advancing economically—is discouraged.

Outright product bans are detailed below. However, even if products are not banned outright, restrictions or tariffs can increase incentives for black markets to develop to avoid incurring additional costs, or to capitalize on opportunities to (illegally) increase revenues. As noted above in **Column N** (protests) the *removal* of tariffs can also be responsible for historical instances of protest by smugglers/black-market competitors of legal importers (Re: Boston Tea Party).

Bans/Prohibition and Violence. Some policy interventions banning certain goods, services, and labor for which there is demand unwittingly can result in a form of entrepreneurship in black markets.

What is generally overlooked in policy proposals to ban products is what happens to the *price of that product —on the black market*. Because bans can result in *supply shocks* (sudden drops in the supply of the goods) or reduced supply overall, huge *price spikes* in the good can result, *making the illegal activity very lucrative* (i.e. economic distortions towards high returns relative to cost). This gives black market businesses an *added incentive* to supply what the policy attempts to prevent. Black market operators/smugglers therefore may even take to lobbying for bans to preserve their highly-paid illegal business activities.

Violence. Bans/prohibition can be the origin of a significant amount of violence, as competition between rival black-market operators heats up. The example of illegal drugs or prohibition of alcohol (U.S. 1919-1933) and the associated gang activity and violence is detailed below because of its role in many forms of violence. Note that the violence is not limited to humans—it can be against *animals* and wildlife such as in the ivory and rhino horn trade, to be noted further below. In this case the black-market suppliers (and perhaps distributors) are referred to as *poachers*.

Illegal Drugs/Alcohol. For example, in the case of illegal drugs, black market operators (e.g. drug lords, or during prohibition of alcohol *bootleggers* of *moonshine* gain considerably from the existence of banned markets, and are also at considerable risk of violent confrontations and death.

Distributorships and Legal Contracts. The problem of violence and prohibition might be better understood with the example of a *distributorship* (such as for a beer brand). An entrepreneur purchases the distributorship for a given geographic area (such as a city) which gives them the exclusive *contractual right* to receive royalty income from beer sales in that geographic area. If someone else tries to sell the same beer brand in that city, the distributor can sue the person for violation of the distribution agreement and can legally seek damages.

When a product is illegal, the only way to enforce one's claim over the "distributorship territory" is through violence—essentially eliminating the competition with a death sentence. Therefore, prohibition and bans of products in high demand can be expected to be associated with an elevated risk of violent activity (including street gangs selling illegal drugs or during prohibition in the U.S. 1919-1933*, alcohol).

Political Alliances / Col F. Rent-seeking activity. Prohibition can result in unintended political alliances: In the U.S. case, between illegal traffickers of alcohol (bootleggers) who gained wealth from the product's illegality (**Col D**) and devout church-goers who hoped to legislate morality by banning alcohol consumption.

Increasing Animal and Wildlife Populations. Poachers also have a similar incentive to lobby for laws to make or keep products illegal to *keep supply low* and push up their returns artificially *without incurring the costs* of breeding the animals. They conduct this cost-decoupled business in black markets (Re:

rhino horns, elephant tusks, certain high-value fish, etc.); unintentionally their interests are aligned with very well-meaning international organizations that push for bans that *further* lower the supply.

When the economics of the impact on animal populations is ignored, banning products may superficially seem like the just stance to take because everyone agrees that poaching is bad. However, as with alcohol prohibition and illegal drugs, poachers gain outsized benefits from the high price advantages caused by supply shocks and limited supplies due to prohibition--moreover, poachers can benefit while avoiding *the cost of production* of raising and feeding the animals.

Increasing animal populations through legal breeding and ranching, as well as *3-D bio-fabrication* (e.g. of horns) can raise supply and lowering prices to reduce incentives for poachers to engage in the trade. ((Associated Press in Johannesburg, 2017; Berke, 2016; Re: Pembient). Increasing the population of endangered marine life through legal *aquaculture* can also increase supply and reduce black markets and poaching at sea.

Taxation and Differentials. Some products which are not banned but taxed very heavily in one jurisdiction and less so in another can lead to an opportunity for illegal operators to gain from the *price differential* across the border (e.g. across state lines in the U.S.) Therefore, there is a greater risk of smuggling activity from the low-tax jurisdiction to the high-tax jurisdiction, and related *violence* between competing operators.

Col D Wealth Gains. Although easily overlooked, System 2 security forces/law enforcement may also benefit from larger budgets and resources to combat offenders/violators of these policy interventions.

Bans/Restrictions: Safety/Environmental. The banning of certain products by regulatory agencies due to safety and/or environmental concerns can be the result of rent-seeking but led by a particularly vocal and active group claiming to act in the public interest; or, public pressure can also possibly be initiated by a truly independent and concerned group with no industry ties and no rent-seeking intentions.

For an example that highlights the costs and benefits of banning a product, as well as the perpetuation of *moral hazard*, consider a product in use that may be responsible for saving many lives. Later, after extensive research the product is found to pose certain risks to human health and or/the environment. Private and or public pressure results in a *ban* on the product. Although the harm caused by the product use may be documented and identifiable, the consequences of future product *non-use* are either ignored, or not easily calculable. The question of the consequences of a ban may never be fully answered, but it is hoped that a reasonably safer *and equally effective* substitute can be used in place of the banned product to continue saving lives.

Immunity. The key question arises how to best prevent moral hazard Should an irresponsible manufacturer be brought to justice through liability claims in the courts, or punished through a ban? The business may wish to avoid the costs of paying out claims and therefore favor a ban and public censure, while preparing a new and safer product to be sold in its place. Counterintuitively, the policy and regulatory framework may thus be complicit to some degree in allowing offenders/manufacturers to escape full accountability as well as leaving the door open for future abuses Also see **Sub2.5c**.

Sanctions and Innocents. A policy to enact sanctions against an offending nation, may enjoy considerable political popularity. The outcome of sanctions depends upon the specifics (products, all trade, etc.), but if a trade embargo (blockage) is involved, a major concern arises as to the potential for *innocent victims*. Will the leadership or those responsible for the offensive behavior in the rogue nation be the ones most likely to be punished by the sanctions? Or will it be more likely that the common citizens under that leadership will bear the brunt of the policy? Without access to imported goods and inputs that were previously available from abroad, there may be increased risk of shortages and famine.

Sub2.6a. Food Supply Blockages. Policy interventions of this type can result in temporary shortages or in extreme cases famine. (See separately **Sub2.2b** regarding central control of food supplies as part of food distribution schemes, and zonal, interstate restrictions).

A policy of central control to procure and/or block the food supply may be instituted during *internal conflicts* where government forces are combatting rebels: As humanitarian organizations point out, food can be used as a *weapon* in this manner. The aim is to prevent food from getting to the rebels by shutting off food supply routes and/or officially redirecting supplies procured from farmers. In some cases, delivery points (sea ports, airports) may be intentionally destroyed or blocked to prevent entry. Supplies, including international relief supplies, may be diverted elsewhere or if a procurement system is established, then officials and armed forces may suddenly find themselves in control of vast stockpiles of agricultural produce with a market value; these caches may be repeatedly pilfered or targeted by merchants for resale and redistribution, but *not necessarily* towards the troubled zones. At some point, it may be determined that food distribution via the previous food supply routes is no longer safe, leaving the innocent inhabitants of the areas of conflict to fend for themselves.

Sub2.6b. Regulatory Non-Approval (De Facto Bans). The existence of official regulatory agencies responsible for the approval of drugs and treatments to ensure product safety superficially appears desirable. However, as noted in **Sub2.3b** regulators have a lot at stake and may be extra cautious about approvals. Moreover, there is a strong incentive for *rent-seeking* by competing firms who prefer to restrict the supply of drugs that might cut into their market shares; this might take the form of supplying regulators with studies that point to the dangers of competing drugs X, Y, and Z (and other forms of pressure through *public relations* that could harm the reputation of regulators should the drug be approved).

Particularly troubling is when it can be argued that verifiably reliable products with a long history of safety and regulatory approval by agencies in *other countries* are still rejected; of course, the details of each case may change one's conclusion.

Due to the nature of this intervention, it is altogether possible that a certain number of reasonably safe and effective products that could potentially save the lives of many either be considerably delayed for release or may never make it to the market.

Sub2.6c. Concessions in Exchange for Sovereignty (Free Trade, Tax Harmonization)

Certain concessions or legal arrangements can be proffered in exchange for the surrender of control to a higher administrative authority. The process begins with a promise to promote free trade among smaller administrative units (regions/localities) to surrender some degree of sovereignty to a higher administrative unit. The steps might resemble the *Zollverein Model* (c.1833) which began with *economic unification* before political unity. In a later phase, the free trade zone becomes unified *politically/fiscally* (1871) such that derivative income-based flows (taxes) are redirected towards a higher-level administrative unit (the nation-state; Germany).

Fiscal Union Phase. To secure fiscal union among *nation-states*, legal agreements might be proposed to harmonize or lower taxes within and among administrative units. Eventually, all states are united fiscally and taxes are paid to a central *supra-national authority*.

In additional to the new over-arching political leadership and administration, global firms may also benefit from unification in terms of lower costs. Income-based payers however, might be expected to pay an additional layer of fees to the new entity, and there may be an increased likelihood of loss of local control, autonomy, and decision-making.

SUBSYSTEM 3: Overriding Interventions--Fiat Money

The fiat money of Subsystem 3 is seen as a natural extension of System 2's reinforcing feedback loop for expanded inflows. As deficits and debts mount, income-based inflows (i.e. taxes) may fall short. Fiat money through the financial system and central banking apparatus is a supplemental source of financing that can be called upon to provide additional inflows to continue the operations of System 2.

Asymmetrical Wealth Advantages (Col D). It should be emphasized that an important distinction between a fiat-based money and money backed by a *real asset* (such as gold, silver, or other assets) is that fiat money gives the owner an *asymmetric wealth advantage*: Unbacked fiat money can be used to acquire and accumulate *real assets*. **Col E**: The costs are borne by those who hold the fiat currency as a form of savings over time. Because additional fiat money creation dilutes the currency, there is a likelihood of a decline in *purchasing power* (Re: inflation) of goods and services. (This fiat money asymmetry is also relevant to fiat money cryptocurrencies covered in **Sub3.6b.**)

However, despite the ability to create unlimited quantities of fiat money, at least in theory, Subsystem 3 has systemic limitations; the aftermath of an *overshoot* (**Sub3 Col K**) the reversal phase (**Col L through Col N**) can in extreme cases morph into a collapse, in which defaults may be inevitable. First, this can occur because the accumulated debt is large enough that *debt service* and full repayment become problematic; at the national level, these include *obligations* such as the unfunded liabilities of government-run pension systems to pensioners, or medical coverage for seniors (e.g. Medicare in the U.S.) (Re: fiscal gap; fiscal crisis; Alesina, et al., 2013; Kotlikoff 2015, McKinsey 2015)

Second, at a subsequent point in the feedback loop following the overshoot, the quantity of money-printing required to cover all of the obligations may be insufficient due to the risk of a high or even a hyper-inflation; in extreme cases hyperinflations can reduce the value of the money to near zero (as can be evidenced by newly-issued bank notes of extremely large denominations Re: Zimbabwe 2008; Venezuela 2017: See Gupta, Hanke 2017).

Subsystem 3 Policy Table. The policy table below summarizes the characteristics of Subsystem 3. The table is divided into two major parts: First, the basic information of each policy in Columns A through E including the beneficiaries of wealth transfer (**Col D**) and cost-bearers (**Col E**); second, the phases (Initial, overshoot, reversal) in Columns F through N.

SUBSYSTEM 3 of System 2

III. OVERRIDING INTERVENTIONS with FIAT MONEY FINANCING (Re: Monetary policy with fractional reserve banking)

Sub3.#	A. POLICY INTERVENTION TYPE	B. Level/Scale (primary)	C. Rhetorical Justification	D. Decoupling: Returns portion. Wealth gains via political support. (Income/wealth distorted upwards)	E. Decoupling: Cost portion. Cost-Bearers: bearing the cost (Net incomes/wealth reduced)
Sub3.1	**Reduction of Borrowing Costs (re: financial repression)**	National	Growth/stability	Borrowers	Savers, Lenders
	a. Interest Rate Decoupling (gap)	Supranational		Asset holders	Job seekers
Sub3.2	**Compensation to Financial Institutions**		Growth/stability	Financial system	Savers
	a. Lending cost reduction policy			Lenders/financial	Holders of currency
	b. Fractional Reserves and Expansion Legality			Banking system	
	c. Caps on deposit rates			Banking system	Savers
	d. Loan guarantees		Growth/stability	Financial System	
Sub3.3	**Fiat Money Issuance and Sustained Expansion**		Growth/stability	Borrowers, Asset holders	Savers, Fixed Income
	a. Reserves, reserves rates* policies (Re: IOER policy (2008))			Financial System	Currency holders
⓪	b. Special Case: Back-up financing (War, state finances; Re: moral hazard)		Security	Defense Industry	Currency holders
Sub3.4	**Asset Purchases/Accumulation (Fiat Money-financed)**		Growth/stability	Asset Sellers* *above market value	Savers, Inc.-based payee
	*also see Sub3.2d loan guarantees, Sub1.4c bailouts/corp. welfare				Currency holders
Sub3.5	**Exchange Rate interventions ***		Growth/stability		
	a. currency depreciation/"beggar-thy-neighbor"			Export industry	Importers, consumers
	b. currency appreciation/overvalued currencies			Importers/consumers	Export industry
	*fiat money interventions in international currency markets			of imports/asset&financial	
Sub3.6	**Fiat Money Policy, Extensions and Linkages**				
	a. Demonetization as industrial policy		Growth/Stability	Tech, financial industry	Currency holders
*	b. Cryptocurrencies, alt-coins (leveraging of central bank fiat) *NON-POLICY		n/a or not stated		

SUBSYSTEM 3 of System 2 — SUBSYSTEM 3 PHASES: Hypothesized elevated risk of occurrence (including delayed impacts)

III. FIAT MONEY FINANCING/MONETARY POLICY--Cont

Sub3.#	A. POLICY INTERVENTION TYPE	Phase 1 (Initial) F. Rent-seeking activity	G. Impaired Production/Reduced Income Impacts	H. Shortages (incl. Food crises)	I. Black markets/violence due to contract non-illegality	J. Clustering: Oversupply/ excess. Spec. and competition	Delay 1-Overshoot K. Deficit/Debt (Expend.> Inflows)	Delay 2-Reversal L. Secondary Policies / Impacts (incl. extra-judicial/ state violence)	M. Ownership insecurity (incl. self); hoarding	N. Visible protests/ unrest
Sub3.1	**Reduction of Borrowing Costs (re: financial repression)**									
	a. Interest Rate Decoupling (gap)	1						Lowering of policy rates (negative)		
Sub3.2	**Compensation to Financial Institutions**									
	a. Lending cost reduction policy	1				1c		Bank reforms; capital requirements/stress testing		
						1c asset market bubbles				
	b. Reserves Expansion Legality	1						Deposit Insurance		
	c. Caps on deposit rates			1a		1a		Crackdowns		
				1a loanable funds,		*1c high yield speculation*				
	d. Loan guarantees	1			1b					
				1b moneylenders						
Sub3.3	**Fiat Money Issuance and Sustained Expansion**									
	a. Reserves, reserves rates* policies (Re: IOER policy (2008))	1				1c	1	Official controls	1*	1*
						1c asset market bubbles		Vacant properties; short-sale curbs	*purchasin g power*	*consumer price inflation*
⓿	b. Special Case: Back-up financing (War, state finances; Re: moral h)	1				*or high-yield speculation*	1	Extreme cases: Hyperinflations		
Sub3.4	**Asset Purchases/Accumulation (Fiat Money-financed)**	1					1	Pension, bank bailouts		
	also see Sub3.2d loan guarantees, Sub1.4c bailouts/corp. welfare									
Sub3.5	**Exchange Rate interventions***									
	a. currency depreciation/"beggar-thy-neighbor"	1		1d		1		Crackdowns		
	b. currency appreciation/overvalued currencies	1	1	1e	1	1	1	Crackdowns*	1	After removal
	fiat money interventions in international currency markets	*1d imported goods, inputs*		*1e Foreign currency*				*currency speculators*		
Sub3.6	**Fiat Money Policy, Extensions and Linkages**									
	a. Demonetization as industrial policy									
*	b. Cryptocurrencies, alt-coins (leveraging of central bank fiat) *NON-POLICY									

Sub3.1 Reduction of Borrowing Costs

Interest Rate Decoupling (or Gap). Reducing borrowing costs below a certain rate is a form of *decoupling* in the financial realm, where the official, *policy interest rate* of the monetary authorities is decoupled from the *rates of return* of individual firms (*natural rates*). Historically, policy intended to stimulate economic activity by means of *debt financing* involves manipulation of *policy/bank interest rates* below the theoretical *natural rate*; initially the additional quantities of debt may produce the desired effect of increased activity (a "boom"), but the *reinforcing feedback loop* of this policy intervention later can result in an *overshoot phase* in which returns are insufficient to cover debt service, leading to loan defaults, economic disruption and so-called "busts."

Sub3.1. and **Sub3.2a. Col D**. The apparent beneficiaries of artificially lowered interest rates are those who borrow money. Borrowers include individuals*, businesses and System 2 administrative units desiring a cheap source of financing. However, because artificially lowered interest rates tend to cause the prices of the assets, goods and inputs bought with the borrowed money to rise along with the lower rates as borrowers compete, bidding up the prices of those assets, borrowers may not benefit as clearly as initially thought ---the higher prices simply offset the benefits of the lower borrowing costs. Moreover, later in the cycle the debt burden can become unsustainable, leading to loan defaults and economic disruptions.

individuals also may be given an added incentive to borrow for home purchases through incentives via the tax system (Re: mortgage interest deductibility).

To induce financial institutions to lend at lower rates, central banks must provide certain incentives for those institutions. *Fiat money* (essentially money declared as money without backing other than the *full faith and credit* of the issuing entity) provides a way for financial institutions to be financially compensated by lowering their *cost of funds* often through manipulation of *policy interest rates*.

Sub3.2a Cols K, L Secondary Policies. In response to lower lending costs, borrowings may increase to the point of an overshoot in which debt repayment capacity becomes insufficient and loan defaults rise, putting pressure on banking institutions' loan portfolios that consist of loans to businesses which are in financial distress. In response, the central bank itself may be compelled to further lower its policy interest rate to ease the burden on borrowers. Meanwhile, banking institutions attempt to institute policy *reforms* that aim to offer additional safety cushions and oversight, including *stress-testing* and *capital adequacy ratios*. An example of an attempted reform is to adjust bank capital requirements according to the riskiness of assets held—the less riskier assets require less capital. For example, assets traditionally viewed as less risky have been *residential mortgages* and *sovereign debt* (Re: Basel accords).

Policy-Induced Risks (Basel Accords). A major concern is the proper evaluation of risk; bank reform policies can push banks to become significantly *overweight* in assets that were thought to be traditionally low-risk but later turn out to be particularly toxic. In the wake of financial, sovereign debt crises and debt write-downs (e.g. Greece), residential mortgages and sovereign debt as a solid basis for bank capital may not have the level of safety previously thought.

Residential Mortgages and Sovereign Debt. It is recognized that the focus on *subprime* mortgages (which may have been heavily distributed within tranches of purportedly higher-quality residential mortgages) might have diverted attention from the issue of the *overall safety* of residential mortgages as an asset class. Given the prospects for *long-term job/income stability* of homeowners given the advance of automation, robotics and AI, longer term, residential mortgages as assets may pose greater risks than historically. This concern also applies to adequate sovereign debt repayment which relies upon a relatively stable long-term income tax base; System 2 policies that inherently reduce income through incentives should be re-examined.

Also see the discussion in **Sub3.3** including of *securitization* (of mortgages).

Sub3.2b. Another policy intervention and tool is the legality of *fractional reserve banking*, which allows banks to hold a certain percentage of deposits (Re: reserve ratio) against the loans they grant. In a simplified example, a reserve ratio of 10% could theoretically mean an expansion of fiat money through lending to 10 times the initial deposit amount. (It is understood that many financial institutions may not necessarily have the deposits on hand when opportunities to lend arise, and therefore may seek the required deposit base *after-the-fact*. But the fundamental concept is unchanged that fiat money can be expanded upon a smaller base).

It should be emphasized that fractional reserve laws, in conjunction with fiat money and artificially low interest rates, give the banking system a remarkably significant source of return and wealth concentration decoupled from the costs associated with lending: Once reserve requirements have been met, additional lending can have a virtually costless element to the lending banks. However, currency holders/savers over time are likely to bear the cost through lowered purchasing power, as seen in **Col E**.

For descriptions of bank-led bubble and crash cycles (Re: Austrian Business Cycle Theory) also see Mises (1912), Ropke (1936) and Huerta de Soto (2012).

Overshoot and Banking Crises. The longer-term consequence of the Subsystem 3 policy rewards to the banking system (fractional reserves, artificially low interest rates) is the likelihood of over lending (oversupply of credit) to the point that debts accumulated cannot be repaid, and the *collateral* (assets taken in case the borrower defaults) cannot be sold at an amount sufficient to repay the bank because of *clustering* of asset sales in the bust (Re: clustering)

Because costs are essentially decoupled from return, an economic distortion and reinforcing feedback loop exists that incentivizes excessive lending. The overshoot is typically characterized by *debt service requirements exceeding income* (debt repayment ability) leading to defaults and growth of non-performing loan portfolios (problem loans) for banks; in the worst cases, the final phase may include bank failures and entire banking system crises, as the historical record indicates: From approximately 1970 to

2015, bank crises were found to have occurred 147 times in 114 countries (Sigurjónsson 2015:9); this is indicative of a *systemic* problem.

Secondary Impact on Real Estate Prices and Rental Markets (Col L). A price distortion may develop in the overshoot during and after which non-performing bank portfolios can balloon. A significant portion of non-performing loans include real estate (residential real estate, apartment buildings, etc.). Although the vacant properties might normally be put back on the market for resale or rental, banks may tend to process the transition more slowly in a bureaucratic manner. Moreover, under the influence of policies originating from the real estate industry, foreclosed properties held by banks (*other real estate owned* or ORE properties) may be held off the market and left vacant longer than would otherwise be the case, reducing the supply of available properties for either sale or rent. This artificially keeps the price of real estate or rentals high, benefiting the real estate industry and property owners while renters and new homebuyers bear the (higher) costs. Since many new home buyers are younger couples, these higher initial costs put them at disadvantage in saving money for the future.

Sub3.2c (Col I and L). Rate Caps. A variant of policies to lower borrowing costs (i.e. lower than would have occurred without the intervention), *interest rate caps* (legal loan rates) may be imposed. To compensate financial institutions (particularly in an inflationary environment) this policy may be coupled with a policy of *deposit rate caps*. Both forms of caps are in *effect price controls* on funds (loanable funds and depository funds) in a financial/banking system context. For the harmful impacts caused by price controls in the non-financial real economy, see **Sub2.1a**

Financial Repression. The distortions caused by controls on interest and deposit rates might be shown with a simple example with several phases.

Initial State. Assume an initial phase where inflation is near zero. Banking policy sets (nominal) deposit rates at 5% and lending rates at 8%. This gives banks a margin of 3% (=8% less 5%).

Phase 2. Declining Real Rates on Deposits. If inflation rises to 10% per annum while the policy remains unchanged, banks can continue to pay 5% interest on deposits held, although the *real* rates being paid to depositors are now *negative* 5%. This not only impoverishes depositors and savers with lower income from their savings but they have a *disincentive* to save further as in *real terms* the value of their savings is declining.

Phase 3. Increased Speculative Activity. Due to declining real value of deposits, depositors may reduce their deposits in banks, leading to less *loanable funds* for banks to lend out. Savers also may attempt to find higher-yielding, speculative, risky assets to invest in, resulting in future losses and financial hardship for them should the markets turn against them. (Re: Financial repression; McKinnon 1973, Chandavarkar 1981, Stockman 2015)

Phase 4. Bank Lending Incentives Unabated. As for the banks, although the legal lending rate limit may be insufficient to compensate for inflation rates (e.g. interest rate cap of 8% less inflation rate of 10%=**negative 2%),** if their funding source is from deposits, *in real terms the banks still maintain their margin of 3%* (adjusted for inflation: negative 2% loan interest *less* negative 5% deposit rates=3%).

Phase 5. Credit Rationing (Loanable Fund Shortages). However, as noted above in Phase 3, because of the disincentive for savers, over time the deposit base may decline as depositors seek higher returns elsewhere, leaving banks with less of the cheap deposit-based funding for their loans. Either the banks must find other (costlier and risker) sources of funding or they will limit (ration) their lending activity. As part of a rationing process, loans are more likely to be granted to the more established and less risky borrowers, typically leaving less-established and smaller businesses and farmers with limited access to debt capital.

Phase 6. Black Markets (Moneylenders). At this point, certain entrepreneurial individuals who may know the borrowers well may initiate or expand their moneylending business to bring loanable funds into these underserved areas at *higher rates of interest*. However, these high rates of interest may exceed the *legally permitted limit*, especially if policies are unable to adjust to high and variable inflation rates. These high loan rates are likely to incorporate high inflation rates as well as risk of non-repayment, since certain legal landholding restrictions may prevent the ability of farmers to use their land as *collateral* for agricultural loans.

Phase 7. Crackdowns. Illegal moneylenders who also are subject to *usury laws* may be pursued in crackdowns on their activities. While it is common for the moneylenders to be maligned for their usurious rates, initial distortive policy interventions play an underlying role. To repeat: (1) sustained/high inflation (i.e. fiat money growth of Subsystem 3) and (2) *deposit rate and loan rate caps,* which can be responsible for severe loanable fund shortages seen in Phases 3 through 5 for which the moneylenders attempted to fill a need.

Sub3.2d Col J. *Loan guarantees*, particularly of mortgages, are a way for financial institutions to lend without bearing as much risk of loss (see the term *moral hazard*). If a default occurs, the guarantee may be called upon, increasing the chance of fiat money creation or taxpayer funds being used to pay for a bailout. Loan guarantees can be related to **Policy #4 Asset Purchases** if the guarantor purchases the loans.

Sub3.3. Fiat Money Issuance and Sustained Expansion

The power to issue fiat money is a *legal monopoly* and historically resides with central banks (Re: Bank of England 1694; Sveriges Riksbank 1668), although there may be some legal exceptions in certain cases. The advent of cryptocurrencies adds a new dimension to fiat currency issuance which is detailed in **Sub3.6b**.

Analysis of Cost in Subsystem 3. From a *coupling bond* perspective, there is minimal cost involved in the physical creation of fiat money, at least relative to the denomination of the notes and coins that are minted (Re: Seigniorage). This low cost applies to *high-powered money* (aka *base money*) (Christ 1968, 1979), as well as the commercial banking system's monetary expansion that is pyramided upon the base money (subject to *reserve requirements*; Re: fractional-reserve banking; required reserves; reserve ratio; **Sub3.2b**).

Distortion. This near-costless nature of money creation produces an artificial incentive for the banking system to create money (lend) via fractional-reserve banking and for central banks to finance government expenditures by *monetization* of their debt/obligations (i.e. buying government debt with base money). This source of financing bolsters the reinforcing feedback loop of System 2.

Cost-Bearers. Currency is diluted by the creation of additional currency units, and holders of that currency (e.g. savers/depositors) bear the costs in the form of reduced *purchasing power* of the currency (Re: price inflation). It is recognized that the growth of the money supply may not necessarily have an *immediate* one-to-one correspondence with price inflation, but over extended periods, monetary expansion can affect purchasing power and inflation.

Financial and Banking Crises. The underlying distortive role of (near-costless) fiat money creation, fractional-reserve banking and interest rate manipulation in incentivizing excessive lending/over-lending can lead to subsequent financial and banking crises (Mises 1912; Huerta de Soto 2012; Sigurjónsson 2015; Re: Austrian Business Cycle Theory). Also see the overshoot phase **Col K** in which the *debt service capacity* of borrowers is no longer sufficient, leading to defaults, bankruptcy, and troubled bank loan portfolios.

Banking Reform Attempts. It is argued that systemic crises, panics, and bank runs can be adequately controlled by various measures including: Regulation of commercial banks (e.g. capital adequacy/capital ratios), the provision of *deposit insurance*, and intervention by central banks as *lenders of last resort* (e.g. bail-outs) to commercial banks. Reinstatement of the original or a modern variant of the Glass-Steagall Act of 1932 is also proposed in order as part of reform proposals following the financial crisis of 2008. However, there remains a question whether incentives would improve towards prudent lending and banking practices by re-establishing a regulatory barrier between commercial and investment banking; if the underlying fundamentals of fiat money creation including fractional-reserve banking and policy interest rates are left unaddressed, the reinforcing feedback loop of credit creation and overshoot (**Col K**) may remain largely unchanged.

See Subsystem 3's **Col L** for examples of policies designed to backstop the consequences of a fundamental distortion of incentives, as well as **Sub3.2a**.

Securitization vs. Credit Standards. It has been argued that financial crises are caused by *securitization* of mortgages (Re: *financial crisis of 2008*; *subprime mortgage crisis*). However, the packaging of mortgages into securities is not necessarily the origin of a financial crisis if the *underlying fundamentals of credit* are respected; the importance of *lax credit standards* including lending to non-creditworthy borrowers cannot be underestimated. Moreover, and critical, are *policy origins* of excessive mortgage lending as detailed here: Reinforcing feedback loops created by fiat money creation and fractional reserve banking, interest rate manipulation, and bank reform policy that may have contributed to the compounding of risk in bank portfolios due to perceived low risk of mortgages and sovereign debt, see **Sub3.2a Cols K, L Secondary Policies.**

Accounting Standards. Moreover, accounting standards that apply to the banking industry may belie the value of their credit portfolios. The role of accounting in the bank financial reporting is also considered crucial; elements of *fair value accounting* (also Re: *mark-to-market accounting* or M2M) tend to be politically unpopular with the banking industry ((Re: FAS 157/Accounting Standards Codification (ASC) 820; Johnson and Leone, 2009). Also refer to **Sub3.4**.

Secular Distortions. The long-term growth of fiat money may tend to push prices higher both by inflating *asset prices* as well as lowering the purchasing power of currency. Over a 10-year period at a 7% rate of inflation the same item will double in price; this price is the *nominal* price which reflects the debasement of the currency over time (currency dilution). Those who bear the cost of this sustained intervention would tend to be holders of cash (currency) that is being depreciated in value through the fiat money expansion process. Some distortions that can develop in capital markets through the systemic phases are noted below.

Sustained expansion of fiat money keeps in place an environment of *financial repression*, previously detailed above in **Sub3.2c**, and which create distortions in loanable fund and deposit markets that impoverish savers and depositors or put them at risk of losses from speculation in the search for higher yields.

Excessive Speculation and Clustering Activity (Col J). Over time, fiat money expansion and the secondary policies of further lowering interest rates can lead investors to seek higher yields. For example, investors may flock to *junk bonds* (high-yield debt) by low policy interest rates. This clustering activity bids up the prices of the bonds and progressively lowers the yield on those bonds (*inverse relationship* between bond prices and yields).

This pricing distortion means that the reality of the risk embodied in those assets is not being properly reflected in their price and yield. This false signal induces new (and perhaps less informed investors) into the market having seen recent gains in the price, and additional debt issuance by firms encouraged by enthusiastic buying. This distorted dynamic eventually can lead to a clustering of losses for investors as the risker firms default (also see **Col J**).

As a *secondary policy* (**Col L**) it is likely that central banks may attempt to intervene in these markets to mitigate losses for institutional investors and "stabilize" the market, but the original distortion caused by the previous policy results in additional distortions in a reinforcing feedback loop, with more bailouts, asset purchases and secular dependence of financial markets on central banks (**Col L**, also see **Sub3.4**) (See Stockman 2013, BIS 2015)

Negative Interest Rates. Eventually, as seen in **Col L**, central banks may push debt markets towards negative yields in their efforts to buy up bonds by bidding up their price, notably *government debts*. (Recall that debt securities are assets to investors/creditors). Remarkably, bond traders/speculators can continue to earn *capital gains* and thereby maintain the market provided that the negative yielding securities become *more* negative!

This distortion and clustering problem also applies to *pension funds* that as part of their asset-liability management (ALM) must match the *duration* of their asset mix to their long-term obligations to pensioners and other investors. Mortgage-backed securities (MBS), with their *negative convexity* can offer a solution as a long-term asset with a higher yield potential (provided that the non-linearities of negative convexity can be managed). However, even if the complexities of ALM and MBS are understood and losses can be avoided initially, the *clustering* of activity induced by lower policy interest rates produces a new and feedback effect with the opposite outcome of that intended: An excess of funds is now bidding up MBS, *lowering* the yields and raising the risk of an ALM mismatch that could still lead to losses that impair pensioner and retiree future incomes.

As losses mount, is likely that central banks will be called upon to purchase many of these securities as well to help bail out troubled pension funds in delayed phases of the subsystem feedback loop. (Also re: underfunded, unfunded pension liabilities).

Price Volatility and Trading Activity. Sustained central bank interventions into capital markets, including for the purchase of stocks and ETFs (exchange-traded funds), also have the effect of depressing volatility and trading activity, leading to shrinking trading volume with possible liquidity impacts, as well. (See Takeo, et al. 2017; Re: financial market distortions, Japan focus).

Zombification. The fiat money financing and role in bailouts, asset purchases and artificially low interest rates also give rise to the phenomenon of *corporate zombies* and *economic zombification* which are touched upon in **Sub1.4c**. The costs borne of each policy as shown in **Col E**.

Sub3.3a. Reserves Rate Policy. An important development in central banking since the financial crisis of 2008 is the policy of paying *interest (rates) on excess reserves* (IOER)-- as of mid-2017 at 1.25% in the United States. This rate serves as some *disincentive* for the banking system to lend out funds into the economy since the excess reserves earn interest. This policy is particularly relevant as central bank assets have ballooned through the 2nd decade of the 21st century following the 2008 crisis, and should massive fractional reserve lending resume, the likelihood of inflation rises considerably.

Feedback loop Modifier. Therefore, the IOER policy may be thought of as a new type of "control valve" that can temper the reinforcing feedback loop of fiat money and fractional reserve banking and potentially slow the process of excessive lending/debt accumulation.

Addressing the economic distortions originating from Subsystem 3 and monetary central planning may be in order. As some commentators note, the level of funds necessary for a future bailout may be unattainable; we may be at a policy crossroads that will require economic solutions that depend less on the role of central banks (El-Erian 2016; Rickards 2017).

Sub3.3b Back-Up Financing (War, State financing). Because taxation (income-based fees) alone may be insufficient to finance additional defense expenditure, central bank fiat money can help keep funds flowing for the war effort. During wartime, policy redirection of productive activities towards industries deemed vital for the war effort (**Sub2.3c Directed Production**) coupled with price controls (**Sub2.1a**) can lead to shortages of certain goods and secondary policies of rationing (**Col L**).

Moral Hazard: Potentially Dangerous Outcomes. While there might be support for the financing of a war such as World War II's fight against the Nazis, there is a highly disturbing dimension of the ability of state finances to receive funding through fiat money. Fiat money can soften the consequences on state finances of bad policies that impoverish cost-bearers (via lowering their incomes) which in turn reduces income-based (tax) revenues for central governments; in this sense, fiat money spawns a potentially dangerous form of *moral hazard* that can lead to a positive feedback loop of *repeatedly* destructive fiat law and policies. This cushioning effect on state finances also can apply during financial crises and crashes following policy-induced asset market bubbles (also see **Sub3.3** and **Col J**).

In extreme cases, this moral hazard could extend to cushioning the impact on the state of large-scale policy atrocities such as relocations and genocide (See **Sub 2.2b**, **Sub2.4d**)

Sub3.3 Gains and Cost-Bearing Detail.

Col D. Financial industry entities are likely to be the beneficiaries of Subsystem 3 policies. To the extent that the activities of System 2 (e.g. governments) are financed with fiat money, all those employed or that are contracted with governments have a distinct income (derivative inflow) advantage.

Col D and E: Firms and Job-Seekers. Lower borrowing costs may incent private businesses to borrow to invest in labor-saving capital equipment, raising returns but impacting negatively on employment *more rapidly* than would have otherwise been the case. (noted in **Sub3.1a** policy table concerning policy interest rate manipulation).

Col K Overshoot. Private businesses can borrow cheaply but excessive debt accumulation relative to debt service capacity can lead to more defaults and bankruptcies than would have otherwise occurred.

Sub3.3 Asset Holders: Long and Short-Term Considerations. The fiat money impact is possibly cumulative and felt over longer periods of time. For assets held long-term such as real estate and possibly long-term business ownership and holdings of quality "blue-chip" stock holdings, the benefits can be substantial in terms of asset appreciation.

Borrowing. Some asset acquirers borrow prudently such that they can continue servicing the debt over long periods and retain the asset(s) without defaulting on the loan and being foreclosed upon. The long-term appreciation of the asset(s) *through sustained expansion of fiat money* may give these borrowers a significant advantage towards wealth accumulation via (prudent) borrowing against assets, compared to those who did not borrow at all.

Stock Buy-Backs. Low interest rate environments allow firms to buy back shares with cheaper debt, report improved earnings per share (on a reduced number of shares), and boost dividend payments on (those fewer) shares, benefiting shareholders and notably, owners of *dividend-paying stocks*.

Wealth Inequality and Reversals. For financial and real assets that are held shorter-term, it is possible that asset bubbles can give asset holders an *initial* wealth effect (in terms of capital appreciation/asset value growth).

Initially, this transitory impact may bring forth criticisms of the disproportionate rise of *wealth inequality* which may be justified at least temporarily (although often the fiat money/monetary origins of wealth inequality may be overlooked). (Piketty 2014)

However, should the overshoot result in a market crash much of that paper wealth can be expected to evaporate, with a likely reduction in (relative) inequality.

Speculative Fervor. Although criticisms may be levelled at those who benefit from a rise in asset markets, it should also be recognized that in a highly inflationary period people may be searching for various ways to *protect the value of their savings*, and therefore are incented to invest in assets that tend to *absorb* inflation as a form of hedge against inflation; this can include stocks, real estate, and precious metals, although potentially with massive volatility in such periods. (Faber 2010; stock market Mexico 1970s-1980s).

Sub3.4 Policy-based Asset Purchases: Impaired Assets. Use of non-market means to transfer wealth is a serious concern with regards to unfair wealth concentration. For example, a central bank (or other System 2 administrative unit) purchases assets that are impaired according to political considerations. If the assets, such as *bad debt* (defaulted, non-performing loans, possibly stock of financially troubled companies, etc.) were simply sold into the System 1 marketplace, bidders on those assets would adjust their value downward to account for loss potential (Re: *credit or asset value write-downs*).

If by policy the asset is purchased at *above what the market value would have been*, this is an *overpayment* that represents a *loss* to those who bear the cost of that purchase [e.g. income-based payers (i.e. taxpayers) and/or savers/currency holders] * The recipients of the overpaid proceeds (the sellers/owners of the assets) have gained wealth by the amount of the imputed loss borne by others. *

***Note:** The relative impact on those who bear the cost varies according to the *mix of the financing*. For example, if fiat money is used to finance a purchase, currency is depreciated (diluted), while if taxes are used to finance the purchase, taxpayers (here referred to as "income-based payers) bear the cost.

The problem of policy interventions to purchase (impaired) assets also relates to *loan guarantees* (**Sub3.2d**) when the guarantees are called upon.

Face Value Purchases. Assets may be purchased at *face value* rather than at a much lower market value. While it is possible for policy to dictate that the impaired assets should be sold at *market values* through a transparent and honest bidding process, political pressures and rent-seeking actors may interfere with this option.

Market-to-Market. As noted above, the banking system is generally averse to adopting a *mark-to-market accounting* approach, which if enforced, could cause a potentially destabilizing downward revaluation of their loan portfolios. (Re: FAS 157/Accounting Standards Codification (ASC) 820). This is not an argument against fair value accounting revaluations based on market price, only that such changes in standards, even if in a direction that more accurately reflects the valuation of assets, can lead to *credit write-downs*. Loan-to-value (LTV) adjustments based on fair value can result in loan portfolios deemed *undercollateralized*. The fear of disruptions to the industry can spark heavy criticism and resistance from the banking lobby and representatives in Congress (Johnson and Leone 2009).

Subsystem 3 Column Detail. Key points regarding the general impacts of policy interventions **Sub3.1** through **Sub3.3** are summarized below according to the most relevant columns:

Sub3.1-3.4 Col E. Decoupling: Cost Portion.

Savers who depend upon *interest income* from savings accounts or fixed income instruments (CDs, bonds) can suffer reduced incomes when policy interventions dictate lower interest rates than would have otherwise existed based on higher rates of return (Re: *financial repression*).

Moreover, fiat money expansion over time can reduce the nominal value of fixed income instruments such as bonds, so that when the bonds mature at face value, the purchasing power of the currency units has declined so that the amount of the face value purchases less than when the bond was invested in.

Sub3.1-3.4 Col J. Asset Bubbles. A problem historically identified by *Austrian economists* and of some concern to central bankers as well is the occurrence of *asset bubbles*, typically followed by asset market crashes and accompanied by massive debt/loan defaults: The types of assets potentially affected are numerous and include stocks, real estate, and bonds. Collectibles including art, precious metals –and in the second decade of the 21st century- *cryptocurrencies*-- also are potential vehicles for speculative fiat money (also see **Sub3.6** fiat money extensions)

Excessive speculation can arise in a low-interest rate environment when the so-called "search for yield" induces investors and fund managers to seek out higher-yielding and potentially highly risky assets (e.g. high-yield or "junk" bonds) to increase their portfolio returns.

Debt Linkages to Asset Markets. The excessive accumulation of debt can trigger crashes in asset markets, as well. *Margin debt* rates, which may be influenced by *policy interest rates,* may not be adjusted upwards sufficiently to discourage further purchases of securities *on margin*. If the market weakens, *margin calls* can trigger mass selling which may produce a cascading effect of further selling, continually reducing the potential proceeds to pay down the debt.

Debt/obligations secured with *asset-backed securities* (ABS) can also trigger a market crash when those assets cannot be relied upon to pay down or repay the debt. For example, highly leveraged investors including hedge funds holding a portfolio of impaired or illiquid assets such as troubled *mortgage-backed securities* (MBS) may be forced to reduce/pay down debt in response to margin call requirements. However, the proceeds from the sale of these assets will be insufficient to pay down the debt. Therefore, they may resort to selling their more *liquid* asset holdings such as *stocks/equities*, the sale of which can contribute to destabilization of *equity markets*.

The problem of *counterparty risk* in *swap* contracts also can severely affect equities when one party goes bankrupt: The position becomes *one-sided* (the previous *net* derivative exposure becoming *gross*) necessitating the sale of assets (e.g. into the equity markets) or some form of *bail-out* to cover the position (Re: LTCM 1998).

Sub3.1-3.4 Col L. Secondary Policies.

Short-Selling Restrictions. To prevent market crashes, governments may also resort to policies *prohibiting short-selling* in the stock markets. Because short-sellers' returns depend upon buying back (at a lower price) the security they have sold (at a high price), this policy effectively removes the ability of the securities to be *bought back as they fall in price*, exacerbating the speed of market crashes as a potential bottom is removed by policy.

Price Controls as Inflationary Response. In extreme cases of high inflation amidst social unrest, governments may also attempt to institute *price and wage controls* which can cause substantial disruptions in production and various distortions (**Sub2.1 – Price Controls**).

Supply Reduction Policy. Following the overshoot phase, policies may be adopted to relax the legal rules governing homeowners' rights on defaulted and so-called "underwater" mortgages, and to forestall foreclosures. This can reduce the supply of potential homes for sale as homeowners remain in possession of their homes; in addition, if banks tend to hold onto vacant foreclosed properties for extended periods, home prices may tend to fall less than had the homes been put on the market.

Sub3.1-3.4 Cols M and N. If price inflation rises sufficiently enough, it is possible for individuals to feel insecure in the ability of their incomes/wages to cover their cost of living as their purchasing power declines; in extreme cases, protests rising prices of necessities and other goods may erupt.

In the overshoot phase, there can be a rise in defaults on mortgages and other assets purchased with debt (e.g. auto loans) as debt repayment becomes difficult. As these assets are repossessed by financial institutions and/or dealerships, the (prior) owners can feel a heightened sense of insecurity.

Sub3.5. Exchange Rate interventions

The interventions in this category generally involve fiat money interventions in international currency markets.

Sub3.5a. Currency Depreciation: Currency depreciation can form part of a national strategy to industrialize through development of *export industries*. Central bank interventions in currency markets lowers the cost of the exported goods in foreign currency terms, helping "sell" the exported products through a form of fiat-money *vendor financing* (i.e. providing credit to the seller). This policy intervention has impacts on foreign competitors who may be less able to compete and consequently suffer declines in their businesses and employment opportunities in foreign countries. When multiple central banks conduct this policy simultaneously to weaken their own national currencies to sell exports, the term *beggar-thy-neighbor* policies or *currency wars* can apply (Rickards 2012).

Sub3.5b. Currency Appreciation/Overvalued Currencies: In some phases of industrialization policies, artificial currency appreciation can be implemented through a *currency peg* to a major currency such as the U.S. dollar. This type of policy might be promoted as a tool to gain cheaper access to foreign technology, inputs, and financing; this can benefit importers, sellers from abroad, and users of foreign-sourced inputs. However, the impact on *exporters* and the development of export industry can be damaging. The policy also sets into motion a reinforcing feedback loop that bids up asset values in the country as well as contributing to the growth of debt both domestically (Re: credit bubbles) and vis-à-vis foreign creditors (Re: foreign debt).

From the perspective of overseas investors, the currency appreciation creates the impression of rising asset values when denominated in foreign currency terms. Confusing the currency-related value rise with rapid economic growth, both local and foreign investors may be enticed to invest in real estate, stock markets and business ventures, in the expectation of future growth. Countries with currency pegs require foreign exchange to maintain the peg (by buying up their home currency with foreign currencies, they maintain the value higher); therefore, foreign capital is needed, including in the form of foreign debt. Currency speculators may ride the trend by placing bets on the rising currency, further causing the value of the currency to rise in a reinforcing feedback loop. Since rising asset values (particularly real estate) and investor enthusiasm form the basis for increased lending using those assets as collateral, debt may tend to accumulate both in-country as well as through borrowings denominated in foreign currencies (foreign debt).

At the point of overshoot in which income is no longer capable of covering increased debt service, financial troubles and bad debt can trigger asset market collapses and bank failures along with the collapse in the value of the currency: Foreign exchange is depleted as investors stung by losses exit, and foreign creditors (those who lend foreign currency) slow or stop their lending. The countries may be forced to *remove* the peg, causing sudden depreciation in the domestic currency value and potentially significant domestic price rises, including for imported goods upon which the economy may have become more dependent in the previous phase. The likelihood of protests from the public/consumers suddenly faced with sticker shock may increase (**Col N**). (Re: Asian Currency Crisis 1997).

Official Exchange Rates. When currencies rapidly depreciate, *shortages* of foreign exchange are felt because increasing amounts of the domestic (local) currency are needed to acquire foreign currencies. In response to pressure from importers and other interests, the government may institute *official exchange rates* to secure foreign exchange at preferential rates. A *black market* of illegal money changers may arise to provide foreign currency at rates that bypass these official exchange rates. This is likely a by-product policy (**Col L**) resulting from earlier policies (excessive government spending relative to receipts, covered by outsized fiat money creation). (See **Sub3.3 Col L** fiat money sustained expansion, official controls).

Sub3.6 Fiat Money Policy, Extensions, and Linkages

Sub3.6a. Demonetization as industrial policy. This category applies to policy interventions designed to modernize a country by reducing dependence on physical cash. Policies encourage more use of digital means of payment such as credit cards, debit cards and various electronic payment systems. With the goal of developing the economy's tech sector and to track transactions for taxation, some countries may attempt some policies to make the use of cash more inconvenient or to demonetize the currency. (Re: demonetization India, 2016).

In a complete change of currency, the intended beneficiaries may well be the financial and tech industry, as well as the public sector, and the victims are those who were unable to exchange the old notes for new notes in a timely manner; if the demonetization deadline is very short, individuals outside of the country or unable to access their cash reserves at the time can find themselves penniless. Moreover, the public is forced to act quickly, leading to long lines, distress, and possible public disturbances at banking institutions.

Sub3.6b. Crypto-Currencies and Alt-Coins. This category is added within Subsystem 3 but is *not* considered a policy intervention per se. Crypto-assets provide a vehicle for existing national fiat currencies, to be explained below. This new category of fiat refers to digital or *cryptocurrencies* and *alt-coins* traded and used as a means of payment typically using *blockchain* technology, beginning with Bitcoin (BTC) in 2009 and other cryptocurrencies such as Ethereum, Litecoin, Monero, etc., as well as countless *digital tokens* that are being issued through ICOs (*initial coin offerings*, often through the Ethereum platform).

Most of these currencies are *fiat* in the sense of having no asset backing, but some are backed (at least in part or in theory) by gold and other assets. An important distinction between a fiat-based money and money backed by a *real asset* is that fiat money gives the owner an asymmetric wealth advantage: Unbacked fiat money can be used to acquire real assets. This of course applies to central bank fiat money, as well.

Although cryptocurrencies and digital tokens are not policy interventions, they may have at some point a significant linkage to the existing fiat money system of central banks in the form of *leverage*. This means that a single fiat dollar of say, Bitcoin, can be leveraged through the cryptocurrency's appreciation potentially by thousands of times. Consider, for example, that at inception in 2009 one U.S. dollar bought approximately 1300 BTC; by mid-2017, this single fiat dollar has been inflated into a value of some $U.S. 4 million through Bitcoin. This implies an outsize multiplication of the purchasing power of fiat U.S. dollar for the owner of those BTC without the U.S. central bank having created any more U.S. dollars to do so.

In sum, while cryptocurrencies and digital tokens can be thought of as a part of a decentralized, private monetary system, through the leveraging from the base of central bank fiat money, they also serve as a vehicle for *additional* central bank fiat money creation without the central banks necessarily having to create excessive quantities of their own fiat money!

If so, this would have the possible *beneficial effect* of stabilizing and reducing the likelihood of inflationary or even hyperinflationary events from excessive creation of national or supranational fiat currencies by central banks. Inflations (and crashes) are also to be expected to occur in countless crypto-fiat currencies, each with their own features and private monetary policies. Fiat cryptocurrency monetary policies can restrain the supply of the currency (built into Bitcoin monetary growth policy, for example); thus, there may be an argument, albeit perhaps weak, for a "safe haven" potential for certain exceptionally reliable, surviving crypto coins that give the owners of these currencies the option of escaping hyperinflations caused by their home country's central bank fiat currencies. Nevertheless, extreme volatility and lack of liquidity, frauds and scams, theft, and *over-tokenization* point to the likelihood of many crypto assets and alt-coins becoming worthless and causing untold losses for their holders (Russo 2017; Spitznagel 2017).

At some point in the future, given the risk of national governments defaulting on their obligations and inability to continue paying out subsidies following the overshoot phase it is possible that by then there might be alternative legal frameworks and impetus for local communities and newly defined jurisdictions to issue their own competing currencies and even shares (equities) to develop alternative financing methods for their business or organizational activities.

***

APPENDICES

PERSPECTIVES
A1. Prices, Costs, and Loss
A2. Ideology, Morality, and Political Systems
A3. Wealth Accumulation: Alternative Scenarios

Appendix 1. Prices, Cost, and Loss

This Appendix provides additional detail and illustrations as an extension of **Sub2.1**.

Price controls can be popular with voters as an anti-poverty measure and to increase affordability for consumers. These well-meaning interventions in the pricing system can produce unexpected and counterintuitive results that in extreme cases lead to tragedy, including food crises and famine. Other possible outcomes of controlled pricing are decreased production and income, black markets, losses, and waste of resources. Price controls are typically coupled with *subsidization* such that taxpayers must often bear the cost of these policies. An unintended consequence is that the poor may unknowingly be taxed to subsidize the controlled prices that they pay as consumers.

Fairness Policy Interventions. Political candidates can gain support by promising to fix prices of necessities. While politically popular, the consequences for production and supply of goods can be disastrous, although not initially obvious. (**Col C** summarizes rhetorical justifications for policies including fairness/morality).

Aspiring leaders may also proclaim certain goods to be a "public right" by virtue of their necessity, or naturally a communal good (e.g. particularly *water*; possibly energy). It also might be argued that the good is too important to be left in the hands of profit-making firms and should be handled by officials acting in the public interest. Consequently, in System 2, there may be support for control over (a) the price (Re: price controls or price-fixing by law) on private suppliers; or (b) the entire supply of that good (legal monopoly or industry takeover by System 2 entities—also see Sub**2.2**)

Price Controls and Realities

Those in charge of pricing for price controls (e.g. public officials or bureaucrats) are faced with the same challenges of pricing that are found in System 1: Knowing what the price should be that discourages waste (in both consumption and supply) and losses (related to waste). Price controls distort incentives; the consequences are described below (also refer to columns **H, I, J**).

Types of Loss

While it is often assumed that a price (of a good or service) can be simply be *dictated* to become fairer, what is often neglected is that *at whatever price is set by the authorities*:

(1) someone must still be willing to *supply* that good or service; to do so, the producer/supplier must be able to cover its costs, otherwise losses will result.

(2) Someone must still be willing to purchase the good or service. If no-one wants to, or can afford to, purchase, the producer/supplier will end up with losses.

Losses can be understood in a *financial accounting* sense and through the concept of *opportunity cost*.

In **financial accounting**, *accrual basis* means that revenues are recognized when earned and the costs associated with those revenues are matched to them in the same period. *Cash basis* refers to when cash is received or paid out.

Loss: Accrual and Cash Basis. It is possible for a firm to be profitable (positive return) on an accrual basis (Revenues>Expenses) while suffering *cash flow losses* as when a company has a build-up of receivables or *unsold inventory*. On an economy-wide scale this *clustering* of excess inventory from overproduction is also referred to as general gluts or oversupply.

For policy origins and nature of clustering, refer to **Col J** and **Sub3.3**.

Since the producer may still appear profitable on its *income statement*, Revenues less Costs comparison should also be considered from a *cash flow* standpoint; this can be seen in the *cash flow statement* of a business' financial statements.

Loss in Opportunity Cost. Loss also includes the cost of *opportunity cost*, which is what one loses by doing something. Therefore, it is possible that a producer could be operating at both a cash flow and accrual profit but *relative to other opportunities* the producer is sustaining a loss in terms of *opportunity cost* (lost opportunity to make a better rate of return elsewhere).

A historical analysis of pricing policies in agriculture suggests that due to disincentives to produce policy-controlled crops (i.e. *food crops* were subject to price controls) there was a gradual shift in land-use patterns away from food crops towards *cash crops for export*, depleting domestic food supplies and contributing to food shortages. (Lofchie 1978a)

Market Logic: Economic and Political

The logic of selling in a market (or at an auction) may explain how prices and pricing work in the absence of price controls. This can be compared with a political marketplace.

Economy. While it is reasonable to assume that producers of goods hope to sell at higher prices rather than lower prices, they must make guesses as to possible selling price points. Ultimately, however, they must rely upon consumers (voluntary buyers) who in the end decide whether to buy.

Prices can be divided into *offering* or *asking* price (the price which the seller hopes to receive for the item). This does *not* mean that the consumer will *necessarily* buy at the offering price. The *selling* price is the price at which the offer and the bid match and the item is sold.

Phase 1. The *bidding* price or the "bid" is the price at which the buyer (e.g. a consumer) is willing to buy the item. In markets where many are competing to purchase a popular or highly needed item, the *high bid* acquires the item. For a product in high demand with relatively little supply, the winning bid is the highest in that that other potential buyers aren't willing to pay as much.

Phase 2. As evidence mounts that the item is selling at some premium, *would-be sellers* tend to bring more supply to the auction/market. As more items are offered /released into the market in response to the high (previous) selling prices, the balance changes. There might come a point that more is being offered than the quantity that buyers are willing to buy. At that point, bidding prices may decline and the high bids *still* win but at prices lower than when the supply was relatively scarcer in Phase 1.

Political Markets. Candidates aspiring for political office/power also operate in a marketplace. The concept of *rent-seeking* has been covered in the main text, whereby certain groups sell their votes (democratic context) or support/allegiance (non-democratic) in exchange for certain favors/privileges to be granted once the candidate attains power. The candidate buys the votes of the rent-seekers; the candidate who bids highest (promises to grant the most favors) gains popularity and wins the office.

Morality of Markets: Economic and Political. It is often argued that economic markets are unfair because someone who really needs the item cannot obtain it at the price paid by the highest bidder. This is particularly relevant in the context of natural disasters when the prices of certain necessities can skyrocket, giving rise to accusations of *price-gouging,* and calls for policies to control prices.

While superficially the argument appears to be grounded in fairness, a moral argument must also consider **Phase 2** as described above. A high price at which certain necessities are sold signals a need which should be transmitted to other would-be suppliers to bring more of what is needed. Moreover, the high price also sends a signal to *conserve* upon the badly-needed resource so that supplies do not diminish too rapidly. The key point is that various options towards supplying people's needs should be allowed. This includes a vital role for charitable and volunteer efforts that can be a lifeline should shortages be exacerbated by price controls.

Crisis and Continued Supply. Price controls can cause distortions such that vital resources are overused and shortages are precipitated. In a crisis, if a greedy business sells at inaccessibly high prices, shutting out 50% of potential buyers, the question of the existence of potential competing supplies must be raised. A major concern is that when price controls become law, supplies may tend to dry up* and stores may close. The strong desire to do the right thing is universal, but how is denying additional supplies to reach those in need moral? Moreover, while it is natural to seek political solutions in the name of fairness and the public good, is it right that policies causing irreparable harm have no consequences?

*an exception to supply interruptions might be *illegal operators* (Re: black markets selling at prices *higher* than the mandated price control; see **Col I** and **Sub2.3**a, **Sub2.4c**, **Sub2.6**, and elsewhere in this appendix).

Asymmetry in Cost-Return. A critical problem with sole reliance on political markets is cost-return disproportionality. When firms set prices that fail to reach all potential buyers of their product due to affordability, *they have lost an opportunity to sell more*. What would cause such a pricing decision? Is it equivalent to a fiat law price control set by a lawmaker in a political market? In economic life, the role of *cost* as a limiting factor in supplying goods and services can easily be underestimated or overlooked: Producers/suppliers must bear costs to supply markets.

In contrast, lawmakers must also produce, but in a political sense: Production of laws that help maintain their popularity towards election (or re-election); this includes legislation on price controls as a display of promoting fairness. However, they are unlikely to bear any cost if their price controls are responsible for shortages of supplies for those in need.

Antifragility and Political Markets. Politics may tend to promote selective *antifragility* in that *gain*s from policy actions are disproportionately greater relative to the *losses* – i.e. policymakers (as well as their consultants and advisers) lose less from their policies than what is gained because they are insulated from the consequences (Taleb 2012, 2016b; *antifragile, skin in the game;* White 2013).

Policy and Cost-Return Disproportionality. A critical point regarding cost-bearing by firms supplying markets is that as rent-seekers, they may lobby for restrictions on competitors through regulatory bans and restrictions (**Sub2.6**). This *reduces the supply* and allows for their prices and the costs of their product(s) to rise more than would be the case without the policy intervention (Re: *EpiPen*, regulatory restrictions; Herrick 2016).

An ancillary role may also be played by the system of *third-party payments* which may allow for higher pricing of certain medical products than would have been otherwise possible with direct payments. For discussion on third-party payment, see **Sub1.1a**.

Distorted Prices (and Costs): Examples

Price Controls and Loss. Although not necessarily conventional, a practical way to think about whether prices are artificially set "too high" or "too low" is whether producers can continue producing without *loss*; types of loss were detailed above.

Lower prices, higher costs and losses send a signal to "slow down" production/supply; high prices, lower costs, and profits (returns) do the opposite.

Ignoring pricing signals means the likelihood of *losses* for the businesses that supply the good; losses are a crucial signal of costs exceeding revenues, inducing producers to slow down production.

Note: For individuals, the same concept applies: losses appear as excessive spending relative to income.

Why would producers sustain losses? Prices and costs reflect a complex interwoven combination of *consumer demand* including tastes, *subjective values*, incomes, *costs of the inputs* to produce that good, and cost in time. Prices are also expected to be in flux, or nearly *constantly changing* in response to changes in overall conditions. Pricing policies as will be seen below are highly inflexible and can lead to losses when conditions change—which is almost always.

Subsidies. As will be seen below and in **Sub1.4** subsidies to firms is a common policy linked to price controls. Although it is common to assume that profit-seeking activities cause waste, the dynamics of price controls and subsidization are rarely understood.

Note: Pricing Policy in Renewables. See the example in **Sub1.4** where subsidies supporting higher prices for renewable resources relative to non-renewable resources lead to a remarkable *overuse* of non-renewable resources to produce and sell renewable resources at the higher subsidized price at taxpayer expense (subsidies).

Shortages and Losses (Prices set too low). Price controls that fix prices artificially low can be a popular vote-getter and viewed as a noble anti-poverty measure. However, the potential for catastrophic consequences is often overlooked.

At a price fixed *too low* consumers understandably want more rather than less, raising the risk of consumer overuse and waste of the resource. To meet a higher quantity demanded by consumers, suppliers must *continue* to supply them at that fixed price (note that the *quantity* purchased is also a cost to the business as an *input*). However, at the low fixed price, the producers may begin to operate at a loss, both in terms of inability to cover costs (Revenues<Costs) but also in terms of *opportunity costs*.

Shortages, Long Lines, and Rationing. *Shortages* may occur because of price controls set too low. As supplies shrink, long lines (queues) can become an unpleasant fact of life. It is also possible that producers (including farmers) may cease production entirely (**Col H**). Secondary policies such as *rationing* (odd-even days, watering days, etc.) may be imposed (**Col L**). Refer to **Sub2.1a** for extreme cases where price controls not only lead to shortages but to food crises and famine.

Subsidization of Losses. It is likely that the popularity of such policies with consumers will induce officials to maintain prices artificially low. Since firms (including farmers) cannot continue producing indefinitely at a loss, they may seek relief through the political process, lobbying for compensation through subsidization. This will allow them to continue to supply the goods cheaply *and at a loss* with taxpayers bearing the cost.
Overshoot. A major risk at some point is the cost of subsidization which can eat into the finances of the government and agencies providing the subsidies. The reinforcing feedback loop can result in budget shortfalls leading to cancellation or severe pullback of the subsidization policy. The removal of subsidies can be in part responsible for protests as described in **Col N** (it is recognized that not in all cases protests can be expected to occur, only that the likelihood of unrest may increase in combination with other policies and actions taken by an increasingly unpopular government/leadership.

Oversupply/Waste and Losses (Price Supports=prices set artificially high). Artificially high prices are often associated with a policy of *price supports*. Here, waste occurs from *the supply side* as the price support encourages more supplier production than can usually be sold, raising the risk of *losses* (Revenues<Costs) with the result being waste in the form of stockpiles of *unsold inventory** (Re: oversupply, gluts, stockpiles; agricultural price supports).

Also see **Col J** and the commentary above explaining the difference between accrual and cash flow losses; in this case, the build-up of inventories represents *cash flow losses* (although due to subsidization explained below producers pass on the losses to the taxpayers.

Subsidization of Losses. Because firms (including agribusiness and farmers) cannot continue producing at a loss indefinitely, artificially high price supports are typically associated with a second policy: *subsidization* (See **Sub1.4a-subsidization of firms**) Because the producers cannot sell enough goods into the market at the supported price, they lose money unless they can receive (government) subsidies to continue producing. The result is typically the build-up of stockpiles of unsold inventory (Re: agricultural price supports) paid for (but not bought) by taxpayers.

Policy By-Products

Black Markets. Both price control policies described above can give rise to black markets, in different ways. Subsequent crackdowns against black market activity are a likely by-product as detailed in **Col L**.

Arbitrage and Subsidized Prices. The price controls intended to lower the cost to consumers give rise to an arbitraging opportunity for enterprising merchants to purchase large volumes of the product at the low controlled price and resell them in other zones at higher prices (either controlled higher or free market prices). This can aggravate shortages in some areas of a country while supplies are abundant elsewhere, including abroad if the goods are shipped across borders.

Price supports: Another source of supply may emerge: Illegal competitors who attempt to supply goods at a price *below the legally fixed price*. This results in more unsold inventories for the subsidized producers while taxpayers continue to pay.

Monopoly/State Control. Subsidization was noted above as a means to compensate money-losing producers whose products are subject to the price supports. Another possibility is that policy may shift towards substantial government control of the entire industry, particularly if most of the production is being sold to the government. However, since losses are no less a threat to state-owned enterprises/legal monopolies (see **Sub2.2**), taxpayer funding of the losses is expected to continue, although this source of funding may no longer be referred to as subsidization, simply part of the state enterprise's annual budget allocation.

Pricing, Conservation, and Loss. As seen above, price controls have serious implications for *conservation* from an environmental standpoint. A rising price tends to discourage usage by consumers, *conserving upon the resource* and reducing waste by consumers.

A falling price signals to suppliers of the good to reduce production to avoid waste and thereby conserving upon resources.

If a producer/supplier ignores the signal of declining prices and continues to produce while revenues are declining, *losses* are likely to result and which is a signal of waste and overproduction.

Subsidies and Wasteful Production. As seen in the analysis of subsidization, once taxpayers are relied upon to cover losses, the likelihood of wasteful production is greatly increased, as seen in unsold inventories, oversupply, and gluts (also see **Sub1.4a**).

The same logic applies to individuals: A consumer who ignores price signals (i.e. rising prices) and costs can suffer an increased *cost of living* to the point of financial hardship (*losses* in the sense of personal expenses exceeding one's income)

Note: Revenues are typically comprised of price x quantity (PxQ). In the commentary on prices and revenues above, *price elasticities* were ignored for simplicity, but their absence from the discussion does not alter the fundamental logic of the impacts of price controls, only the point at which losses might be theoretically incurred. (On price theory see Friedman 1986; Stigler 1987)

Price and Cost: Non-Money Illustration

It can be instructive to eliminate money/currency units when explaining prices so that it is clearer that prices are *exchange rates*.

The following story is split into three parts: The first part illustrates the exchange of production *for time units*: The price in time, and the cost in time. The second part shows the exchange of one's production for someone else's production: The price in trade. The final part shows what happens after investing in time-saving technology.

1. Producing Without Trade

Price and Cost *in Time*. Time is embodied in everything. On average, I catch 5 fish in a day (averaging good and bad days), the *price* of catching (producing) **1 fish** *in time* (a day) is 0.20 parts of a day or 20% of a day (=1 day/5 fish; a full day is 100% of a day).

I must eat at least 2 fish a day which supplies me enough energy in joules to survive; those 2 fish per day are my **cost** (of living, or of consumption). In terms of time, my **cost of living** is 40% of a day; the remainder (60%) is the return (called here a surplus) than can be stored for the future.

Accounting #1. Producing alone:

Cost of Living/day

I eat: 2 fish /day (**Cost in Time**: 40% of a day)

Return/day

Adding to Storage* (as surplus/saved/positive return): 3 fish (Cost in Time: 60% of a day)

Why add to storage? The reasons include:

1. **Insurance**. Just in case of a storm or if I get hurt.

2. **Inventory**. In case I can find something that I want to trade the stored fish for in the future.

3. **Leisure.** To eat on days when I feel like relaxing.

3. **Investment**. To be used to eat on days when I need time to design and build a tool to help me catch fish in less time.

2. Trade/Exchange

Price and Cost in Trade/Exchange. Trade allows me to diversify my diet: I like chicken so if I can find someone who sells chickens then we negotiate what our exchange rate is going to be. But I need something to trade with over my cost of living. Therefore, I need a positive return (surplus), which I have: 3 fish per day.

The Return (Surplus). My daily return is 3 fish (=5 fish caught less 2 eaten). I am willing to trade all of them to get a chicken, but I'd rather keep 1 fish for storage if I can; a little timid, I *offer* 2 fish for 1 of her chickens (i.e. I am offering an exchange rate of 2 fish/per chicken). She says no, she wants 3 fish for one chicken. I agree. **Deal**: **The price** of a chicken now is **3 fish per 1 chicken**.

The cost of a chicken

(a) in terms of fish is **3 fish** per day

(b) in terms of time is 60% of a day.

Supply. At an exchange *rate* (price) of 3 fish per 1 chicken, I sell 3 fish in exchange for 1 chicken *per day*. (Time unit must be included)

Demand. At an exchange *rate* (price) of 3 fish per 1 chicken, I buy 1 chicken for the 3 fish *per day*. (Time unit must be included)

Accounting #2a. After producing and trading:

Cost of Living/day

I eat: 2 fish + 1 chicken (Cost in Time: 100% of a day)

Return/day

Adding to Storage (Savings): *Nothing*

*****Rethinking**: Since 2 fish + 1 chicken is a lot to eat for me in one day, I figure I will try to store 1 fish per day in reserve for future needs (storms, injury, etc.). I usually have enough salt to salt 1 fish per day without extra time being spent trying to mine for salt. The result after reworking the numbers:

Accounting #2b. After producing and trading (+ reconfiguring my diet and saving preference):

Cost of Living/day (Adjusted)

I eat: 1 fish + 1 chicken (Cost in time: 80% of a day)

Return/day

Adding to Storage (Savings): 1 fish (Cost in time: 20% of a day)

3. Time-Saving Technology

Investment* in Technology. Later, I succeed in building a better tool (a big net) and can *double* my daily catch to 10 fish per day. This investment in technology results in an *economization* of time (using ½ the amount of time as before to catch the same amount of fish). This is also called increased *productivity in time*.

Price and Cost in Time: New. Now one fish costs on average just 0.10 of one day (only 10% of a day). This gives me extra time to mine for salt and to salt extra fish that I can keep for storage. I can now eat and more fish per day: 3 fish per day instead of 2 which gives me more energy, then I keep 2 for the storage (just in case) and still have *5 left over to trade per day*: 10-3-2=5!

Next day, same negotiation with the chicken seller. She won't budge on her chicken price so I get one chicken for 3 fish, just as before. But now I still have 2 fish left over for *something else*. Her cousin "T" sells a potato-like root so I get 1 potato for each fish.

The price of a chicken is still **3 fish per 1 chicken**.

The cost of a chicken in terms of

(a) fish is still **3 fish**

(b) in terms *of time* the cost of a chicken has *declined* to only **30% of a day**, ½ as much time as before. This decline is because I have economized on time by being able to catch more fish in the same amount of time (more productive in time).

Accounting #3. After producing, trading, and investing in technology, here is the accounting:

Cost of Living*

I eat:

3 fish + 1 chicken + 2 potatoes (**Cost in Time**: 80% of a day)

Adding to Storage (Savings): 2 (salted) fish per day (20% of a day)

*****Cost of Living: Detail.** My cost of living in terms of time has doubled to 80% of the day from 40%, but because of the economization *in time*, I am able to eat more, enjoy a more diversified diet, and I can *still* store 2 fish each day as a reserve.

I also have the option of reducing my consumption to 2 fish/day and 1 potato/day, lowering my cost to 60% of a day, and increasing my stored amount to 3 fish per day (30% of a day) and 1 potato/day (10%)=Total return of 40% of a day.

We ignore the transportation time to bring the fish to market, plus the time spent mining for extra salt.

Appendix 2. Ideology, Morality, and Political Systems

Policy Formulation and the Social Justice Imperative

A central argument for policy change is the claim that the actions to be taken are moral and therefore justified. Historically, a critically sensitive area has been moral arguments surrounding the *distribution of wealth*. Policies designed to deal with wealth creation and ownership of wealth are largely the result of a moral battleground—who can deliver (social) justice better? The ideologies and political systems that result can become drivers of policy change. A convincing enough ideology can gain adherents and lead to accession to political power and policy change. Fairness and morality are particularly powerful forces for policy change.

Unfortunately, potentially disastrous contradictions between goals/rhetoric and actual outcomes can occur. Also, misguided attempts to explain root *causes* of injustices may be based on misconceptions that when translated into policy, can have unintended consequences. Next, the historical record is examined briefly.

Morality and Fairness Ideologies. Historically, the most prominent ideologies that most *forcefully* pledge to correct for *wealth inequality* (unequal *wealth distribution*) and economic/social injustice have used the *name*[1] Marxism or Communism (Marx 1867). A central and particularly attractive quality of the philosophy that increases the likelihood of gaining adherents is the moral argument that the *absence of profit* (return), solves the problem of social injustice which is deemed to be caused by *profit* and the *profit motive*[2]. (Regarding the broad appeal of targeting wealth, Re: *politics of envy*).

As previously noted, profit cannot be viewed as stand-alone, as it is assumed to be fundamentally linked to the associated cost (cost-bearing); therefore, a legitimate issue should be the fairness of receiving profit (return) when the cost is not fully borne (cost-benefit disproportionality). However, the origin of *cost avoidance* does not appear to be a focus of the analysis of social justice (previously discussed in **Sub2.5b** and **Sub2.5c**, cost transference and judicial immunity, respectively).

[1]*Name*: Although easily overlooked, a critical commonality of *collectivist* ideologies (which includes communism and fascism) exist in the form of labelling and persecution of a group they define as wealthy: *National socialism* (Re: Nazis) justified initial policy actions against a minority (the Jewish people) for their wealth and having purportedly enriched themselves dishonestly and at the expense of others. Also see the commentary on *fascism*, below, and policy **Sub2.4d** in the policy tables for various examples. (Re: Reisman 2014).

[2]Regarding the profit motive and injustice, see the next section.

Analysis of Injustice. From the standpoint of a *coupling bond* concept, it is not possible to determine whether *profit* (return) *alone* is the source of injustice since the return is assumed to be fundamentally bound to *cost-bearing (*the cost borne*)*. What most would agree would be immoral is allowing one person to bear the cost while *all* the return from that effort would be given to someone else (i.e. slavery). The ideological solution devised *at least in theory*, lies in *destruction of the return* so that *even though* the cost-bearers are not permitted to receive anything for their efforts (universally acknowledged as immoral), *no-one else can either*, so the final result of *no beneficiary* is assumed to be *at least fairer*. In a remarkable logic, we are led to an apparently *fairer* form of human slavery. (Re: Lévy, 1977; Hayek 1944)

Exploitation is an important element of social injustice: The capitalist (e.g. factory owner) vs. the worker. An oversight of Marx regarding capitalist exploitation of underpaid workers is the *intertemporal nature of payments* (present vs. future). The workers are paid wages *now* for work performed while the capitalist must wait to receive an uncertain return at some point in the future should the product(s) be sold at the intended prices. While the wages may be considered too low (which may very well be the case, particularly when the impact of inflation is added to compute *real* wages), wages paid also can be expected to reflect a difference (discount) between payment in the present vs. possible payment in the future. (Hoppe, 2006) The uncertainty of the future is also linked to the concept of subjective value and consumer demand, discussed in the section just below.

Fair Share and Theories of Value. In relying on the concept that value is *intrinsically* embodied, including the labor-time invested in making a good/product, Marx built upon the error of the *classical economists* (Smith 1776, Ricardo (1826) in their *labor theory of value*. The concept that value originates from *subjective value* (e.g. consumers and their preferences) emerged later. This painful point can be illustrated by a laborer/artisan who spends many hours creating a fine work, only to find that there is no demand for the item—no buyers. The opposite case might be a popular entertainer or musician who becomes wealthy due to high consumer demand for their works. Due to the subjective valuation of millions of customers and fans quantifying whether the cost borne is truly proportionate may be elusive. However, can costs be borne in another way? For example, if later the entertainer is found to have committed misdeeds will they bear a cost not only in terms of ruined reputation but in the destruction of their future income and wealth?

A similar error exists in using *cost of production* as the basis for value; whatever the item may have cost to produce, if consumers don't (voluntarily) wish to buy it, the value has evaporated. Similar observations were made as early as the 16th century (de la

Calle 1544; Re: School of Salamanca). (Re: Subjective value/imputed value see William Stanley Jevons, Léon Walras, Carl Menger).

Unjust Wealth Accumulation. Another justifiable and crucial point concerns wealth that has been unjustly obtained. The policy tables of the subsystem (**Col D** and **Col E**) indicate where policy can be instrumental in transferring wealth to one party while impoverishing another who bears the costs.

Moreover, rather than relying upon political and *extra-judicial* actions to right wrongs (an approach which is prone to give rise to more injustices and abuse of power due to its overriding and arbitrary nature), the imperfect *court system*, can evaluate claimed injustices on a case-by-case. It is recognized that critical problems must be addressed regarding a biased judiciary that reflects the interests of the politically connected (Re: rule of law; judicial bias; judicial immunity discussed in **Sub2.3d** and **Sub2.5c**).

Briefly, before examining the historical record, a clarification with regards to labels and ideological banners (including "isms").

Rhetoric and Labels vs. Actual Policies. Using names/labels for ideologies (many ending with "ism") is subject to *misinterpretation*, not only because of varying definitions, but also a label can even become associated with another entirely different set of policies over long periods of time. A case in point might be the philosophy of *classical liberal(ism)*, which could be said to contrast significantly with what might be called *liberal (socialism)* or *liberalism* in the early 21st century.

Political system "A" described as "socialist" may have many policies and institutions more closely associated with other political systems that are labelled "capitalist," "Keynesian" or "mixed economy." Political system "B" self-described as socialist may adopt policies with similarities, yet distinct in notable respects from, countries that have historically been described as "fascist" or "communist/Marxist." (Ottaway 1978)

As a starting point, reference to the labels/names of political systems may be unavoidable. But because of the likelihood of confusion it is much clearer if the *actual policies*, rather than the labels, are the focus of study. Moreover, an analysis should consider that, due to the nature and opacity of the political process, leaders might not practice what they campaigned on, and perform a bait-and-switch once in power.

Historical Record of Fairness Ideologies: Theory and Practice. Actual implementation of a goal to destroy all return (profit) requires a massive *transfer of power and intervention into the functioning of society*; therefore, there is believed to be a much higher risk of *despotism* and capricious *abuse of power*.

Moreover, those most closely aligned with the party in power/system's power structure are likely to have privileges that lead to a greater (relative) level of wealth for these politically-connected elites. (Re: *Nomenklatura;* Voslensky 1984)

Arguments that these types of systems were not implemented properly and could succeed if tried again either underestimate or overlook *the universal level of force (and violence) necessary* to destroy any semblance of return (Re: equality of result), which includes state ownership of all property and income. In practice because the system is unworkable without allowing for *some form* of coupling to occur, *black markets* are likely to be an (underground) feature of these economies as seen in the policy table **Col I.**

Later, as the feedback loops created by the policies take effect, the regime may change course towards *liberalization* and eventual abandonment as seen in the Soviet Union on Christmas Day, 1991—in this case, the system lasted for approximately 73 years (which included reliance on black markets). On reconstructing Soviet economic statistics from 1920 to 2015, see Smirnov (2015). For a fictional account of a *totalitarian* society see Orwell (1951).

Other Evidence. In practice, it is expected that regimes under the banner of Marxist/Communist-inspired egalitarianism would tend to adopt at least some policies that are generally consistent with those listed in **Sub2.1 and Sub2.2** in the policy tables.

The subsystem overshoots and delayed phases of the feedback loop phases of countries that tend to subscribe to similar ideologies has been recently observed in Zimbabwe (2008) and in the events unfolding in Venezuela. Many policies develop over decades and a study of the history of policy is instructive; in Venezuela, a significant policy shift arguably occurred in 1958, in 1975 the petroleum industry was nationalized; subsequent fairness-based policies as well as secondary policies under various regimes since have shaped the fate of the country (Re: Chavismo; See Niño, Hanke 2017).

Regarding equity-motivated ideological origins of African hunger (1970s) see Lofchie (1978), Ottaway (1978), Young (1982).

It should be emphasized that in terms of *loss of life* (including genocide by policy-aided mass starvation), the record of countries that have tended to adopted policies involving *totalitarian* or heavy state control-oriented policies during the 20th century have been well-documented (Re: democide, Rummel 1997; Reisman 2014).

Fairness Policy in Other Modern Systems. Broadly speaking, many modern *social democracies* tend to permit much of System 1 to function, with heavy focus on the *redistributive policies* as in **Sub1** with policy interventions that may be sold as advancing the cause of fairness (or safety, etc.) but which can lead to (perhaps unintended) wealth gains for favored groups and firms, especially in the financial and banking industry (Re: crony capitalism). There are various monikers for these systems, all of which have enough similarity that it is more useful to study the policies rather than the names.

These are: *Keynesianism, mixed economy, crony capitalism*; when the exercise of state power is particularly enhanced, the term *fascism* could be applied.

Recall that as stated above, the associations with various names/labels strongly suggests focusing on specific policy interventions. Missing from the list above is *capitalism*, which is due to the extent of interventions in most systems, is not thought to exist, except perhaps in local marketplaces; also, as will be discussed below, *capitalism* is often mistaken for *crony capitalism*.

Overall, the combination of redistributive spending and social programs with highly accommodating central bank financing for much of this activity can be referred to as *Keynesianism*, or perhaps *mixed economy*, a system that underpins many modern democracies of the 20th and early 21st century. This is named after John Maynard Keynes (1936), although the current expanded role of central banking may far surpass his own original framework. Keynesianism is related to *crony capitalism* (which is often mistakenly equated with *capitalism*) which is discussed below.

Many of the criticisms of *capitalism* conflate the term capitalism with *crony capitalism*. Crony capitalism is generally described as private firms working in close alliance with policymakers to benefit from System 2 policies and redistribution. This encompasses all subsystems (Sub1, Sub2, Sub3) and includes taxpayer-funded (government) contracts (**Sub1.2**), subsidies or other forms of *corporate welfare* (**Sub1.4**). (Re: Mitchell 2017b). For crony capitalism in the financial arena refer to Subsystem 3 and Stockman (2013). Without System 2 interventions/taxpayer funding for businesses *crony capitalism* is stripped of much of its unjust powers.

Fairness ideology can also take the form of *the targeting of a minority group* that is accused of being *wealthy*, giving the justification for subsequent policies authorizing wealth confiscation and genocide (Re: *National Socialism*; Nazis; Jews and the Holocaust).
In the U.S., refer to the internment of Japanese-Americans during World War II, many who owned property in the West Coast of the

United States. Regarding policies of forced relocation see **Sub 2.4d**.

As a generalized definition, fascism could be viewed as an extreme version of crony capitalism or Keynesianism through extensive state control and interventionism; it is also assumed that *violence* is more likely to be resorted to, as in communist systems, although unlike communism, *private property* is generally permitted, except for targeted groups (see above).

Fascist systems might be expected to exhibit an especially tight relationship between the national government and (typically, big) businesses towards implementing policies that favor them (also seen in **Col D** Wealth gains). *Fascism* isn't typically associated with fairness policy but historically fascist leaders can appeal broadly to fairness rhetoric in the pursuit of social justice goals, including Mussolini in the 1920s (Goldberg 2009; Sowell, 2012).

Although a close alliance between big business and government also could be said to exist in social democracies, in modern (early 21st century) usage the term *fascism* is more likely to be associated with violence and *nationalism* or *ultra-nationalism*. While government control of the economy with ownership in private hands may rarely be referred to as fascism in modern usage, by whatever name, there is a political advantage to such an arrangement in the ability to shift of responsibility for policy failures onto private enterprise. (Sowell, 2012)

However, nationalism is not considered to *necessarily* presuppose support for any *particular* political system (Re: rhetorical justifications for national security).

Ideologies Advocating Reduced State Intervention. While the above ideologies tend to maintain power and its concentration through rent-seeking and decoupling, there are ideologies that advocate *minimization of state power* and reduced *interventionism* into the economy (Re: free market capitalism, *minarchy*, libertarianism, *laissez-faire* policies; Re: Smith (1776); Mill

(1859); Hayek 1944; Rothbard 1961; Friedman 2001, 2008; McCloskey 2017). Criticism of these types of ideologies and policies focuses on social justice concerns and the threat of anti-democratic despotism in favor of the wealthy. Remarkably, this "threat" may very well *already* describe the status quo; therefore, without addressing the origins of such *existing* concentrations of power that lead to unjust wealth, and without an understanding of the inherent contradiction of fairness policies that produce unjust outcomes, despite good intentions, the problem remains largely unresolved.

Practically speaking, a political candidate honestly advocating for reducing the most troubling elements of interventionism would likely be faced with opposition by *special interests* and *rent-seekers*. Therefore, their goal of achieving something akin to *free market capitalism* truly absent of self-serving concentrations of political power is unlikely; the exception might be at a more *local* level (e.g. local markets) with more personalized customer service to build loyalty and to secure longer-term repeat business relationships. Regarding *capitalism* and critiques see Marx 1867, Rand 1966, Reisman, 1996, Piketty 2014; for commentary on Piketty's work see Taleb 2016b).

Individualism vs. Collectivism. Some advocating reduced interventionism argue that in essence there are only two basic "isms:" *Individualism* and *collectivism*. Although definitions might vary and the designations may be viewed as oversimplified, the basic difference lies in two fundamental approaches:
1. Transferring decision-making and authority away from individuals, to be entrusted with *other individuals*--such as those with greater knowledge, superior moral purpose, and who (claim to) represent the collective will.
2. Allowing individuals to make decisions and act for themselves.

*The latter being subject to generally established rules against *coercion* and *theft* including *fraud*; Re: *Tort law*; Ralph Nader;

rule of law; Aristotle (c. 350 B.C.), Locke (1689); Madison (1788); Sowell (2007); Mitchell (2014); Hanke (2015).

Future Policy Risks
As hypothesized above, the likely outcome of System 2 machinery as exists today will be the direction of funds towards priority special interests and budgets: In particular, pensioners/retirees dependent upon pension income and medical care, and *non-discretionary expenditures* (national defense, pension, and senior medical care obligations) will likely be a dominant force, while recipients of *discretionary budget items* (certain transfer payments and subsidies) will receive less funding.

Pensions and the Overshoot. Underfunded pensions and unfunded pension liabilities, both public and private are a major concern for the future, and which underscores the importance of wealth accumulation and sustainable economic growth.
However, a hypothesized reinforcing feedback loop suggests an overshoot with a troubling outcome. Without proper preparation, many of those who are dependent on transfer payments and other forms of government supplied resources as outlined in Subsystem 1 will be left without sufficient means of support or the proper tools to rebuild their incomes independent of System 2.

Belief Systems. The topic of religion and religious ideology is beyond the scope of this commentary. It can be added however, that so-called "religious fervor" or fanaticism doesn't necessarily have to involve *religion* per se. It is possible for some who reject, or have no connection to, traditional religion, to practice their beliefs in the form of other ideologies and adopted faiths; new messiahs may serve as replacements with the same fervor and intolerance. Typically, positions taken will be firmly based on claims of morality and justice, which can be a form of *virtue-signaling* but also are praiseworthy.
The explanation for socio-economic or other problems may be said to lie essentially in a decline in moral standards (moral

decline); less often pointed to are *underlying secular policies* that can fundamentally alter human incentives, values, and behavior to exhibit such immorality. (Murray 2013). On the quasi-religious facet of Marxism see North 1989; on the theory of *mass movements, collective action,* or belief systems, see Hoffer (1951); Olson (1971); Sowell (1996); Sowell (2002).

Intransigent Minorities. A critical and unresolved concern of modern social democracies is that the overriding authority of fiat law inherently allows access to political power by particularly ideologically-driven and intolerant groups that do not necessarily reflect the majority of opinion-yet the majority submits to their preferences under the "minority rule." The theory of complex systems suggests that a small percentage of the population, up to 3 or 4%, for this effect to take place (Taleb, 2016a).

In extreme cases, the accession to power of a minority can result in violence, conflict, and widespread violations of human rights, including genocide (including through policy-backed starvation) of non-believers, non-supporters, those of a differing ethnicity or race, or those deemed as "undesirable elements" (however defined) (Re: ethnic cleansing, pogroms, holocaust, Rwandan genocide-Hutu against Tutsi, 1994).

Appendix 3. Wealth Accumulation: Alternative Scenarios

This appendix is an extension of the section on **wealth accumulation via compounding** in the description of the characteristics of System 1. Recall the formulas from that section, one for *continuous* compounding over time, $W_t = C_0 e^{rt}$ and the other where the frequency of compounding periods is specified: $W_t = C_0 (1+r)^t$. Several simplistic scenarios are given to illustrate the impact on wealth accumulation of various economic environments.

(1) **Zero Rate of Return**. Assume the initial investment C_0 is 100 and the rate of return r thereafter is 0. Your investment does not

grow and remains the same *nominal* amount of 100. No wealth accumulation in nominal terms.

(2) Negative (Real) Rate of Return. The word *nominal* was used in (1) above because if there is *inflation,* the *real* value of that initial 100 declines in terms of *purchasing power* (what it can buy); in other words, the nominal 100 currency units shrink in *real* value terms. *Taxes* also are a deduction from income and therefore can reduce rates of return.

Note that inflation and taxes are viewed as originating primarily from *redistributive policies* that transfer income and wealth: Taxes/income-based fees are covered in Subsystem 1; subsystem 3's fiat money creation is a form of currency dilution; over extended periods of time, even at relatively low monetary growth and inflation rates, the purchasing power of currency is expected to decline.

Three different cases of rates of return will be compared below in the section (5) below on investing.

(3) Total Wealth Destruction. The next minute after investing the C_0 some event occurs causing a total loss of your investment (theft, confiscation, value of investment goes to zero, etc.); since the investment C_0 itself is gone, any rate of return it could have earned is also gone – in short, *total destruction* of the initial wealth.

(4) Nothing to Invest (Illustration)

The dire case of someone who has nothing (i.e. nothing saved up) can give insights into the essentials of investment activity. The exercise below is not necessarily realistic or accurate, but hopefully provides some clarity by focusing on production in terms of *units of energy* (thus the physics reference) as well as the crucial role of *innovation* in the investment and wealth accumulation process

Innovation and The Physics of Economics. Assume that we can produce a little more than basic subsistence, with some food storage left over: Our daily average calorie intake is 1200 calories or about 5000 joules of energy; anything not consumed is stored for later when possible.

A storm hits and everything has been destroyed but fortunately we are unhurt; assume that we have no friends, family, or community to rely upon. What do we have to invest with? The investment C_0 is the use of three precious resources:

1. Drawing up our *own physical energy*;
2. Economizing on *time as a resource*;
3. Ingenuity/Innovation and skill (Re: *human capital*);

In this dire situation, we draw upon our own energy reserves in each time unit (the day) to find ways to produce for basic survival (subsistence); if possible we also hope to *improve our capacity* to produce beyond basic subsistence.

The Variable C_0 is the *units of energy consumed* (in joules) together with our innovative brainpower and skill as we build tools or equipment to produce more in the same unit of time.

Basic Subsistence ($r=0$). In desperate hope of rebuilding our life, each day nature forces us to draw upon 5000 joules of our *own* energy and our innovative capabilities to construct tools (e.g. net, shovel, extended grabbing tool, etc.) that will permit us to at least produce enough for basic subsistence. These 5000 joules per day with nothing left over implies a *zero* rate of return and no ability to store up additional calories for the future.

Positive Rate of Return. Afraid of living on basic subsistence with no reserves indefinitely, we resolve to find ways to produce 10% more food energy (e.g. fish, roots, nuts, berries, etc.) than the daily 5000 joules we consume for basic subsistence, or 500 joules. If successful by year-end this would equate to a total of 1.825 million joules (5500 joules/day x 365 days) for an average of *5500 joules per day* and a rate of return r of 10%.

Compounded Positive Rate of Return: 10 Years. Suppose that over the years the tools and techniques of production are tinkered with incrementally in an attempt to gain another 10% of food energy *on top of* the previous 10% increase each year. At some point, basic agricultural (aquaculture) methods are introduced and improved upon, as well. If the *r* can be maintained at 10%, *compounded annually* as technological advances are made, after 10 years of annual compounding including the first year of growth of 10% production is now about 12,969 joules* per day, about 2.6 times the initial 5000 joules/day.

*Here the daily average is converted into, and computed from, annual figures (365 days): $W_t=(5000 \times 365) \times (1+.1)^{10}=4.73$ million joules/year/$365=12,969$ joules/day.

This leave us with a *return* (or surplus, profit or net benefit) of about 7968 joules per day over our original basic subsistence.

Wealth Accumulation. Because of the 10% rate of return plus the compounding effect over the 10 years, we produce at a rate such that in less than a day of production we gain an *extra day* of calories to live on. Each month, we gain about 47 extra days of calories to live on, and in a year, we can save up well over a year's worth of extra calories for storage.

Accounting for Costs. The above example ignores the costs of production and therefore the rate of return is a *gross* figure. In conjunction with additional production, there is likely to be an *increase in costs* which is expected to reduce the rate of return considerably below 10%. Suppose that the rate of return *net of costs* is more realistically 7% per year. In a 7% rate of return case, over the 10 years compounded, the average daily production would be about 75% of the 10% case and would have roughly *doubled* instead of increasing 2.6 times.

Options. One might argue that even though the increase in production is impressive, isn't that overproducing and wasteful? What can we possibly do with all that extra production? These accumulated *positive returns*/extra bundles of energy (in the form of whatever has been produced, whether fish, roots, berries, nuts) are not necessarily *all* stored up in a huge pile; the options include: Stored calories can be drawn on in part for future *leisure* (consume the calories on those days and not work); production can be brought to the market to *trade with* (to obtain other items desired in exchange)*; storage is also used for *insurance purposes* (in case another storm comes, or if we get injured or ill).

For items with a shorter shelf life that spoil quickly and cannot be preserved easily, more trade than storage might be necessary; trade for more storable items might be an option.

(5) Investing: Three Cases

Three simplistic cases are examined, with and without redistributive impacts. Case #1 is in *nominal* terms, ignoring taxes* and inflation; Case #2 is in *real* terms that computes moderate taxes and inflation that arise from redistribution (non-fiat and fiat money); Case #3 increases inflation rate of Case #2.

Recall that taxes are also referred to here as income-based fees and derivative inflows into System 2.

Case #1. Nominal: Tax and Inflation Ignored. Assume an investor puts money into a Certificate of Deposit (CD) at 5% interest per annum, compounded daily (365 day). C_0, the initial amount invested (also called an *outflow* here), is 100 currency units. the annual *percentage rate** that the CD earns is 5%. W_t is the *future value*/future wealth accumulated (in currency units) at after a given number of years (t), compounded daily (rounded); the *return* is $W_t - C_0$.

Case #2. Real: Moderate Inflation and Taxes. We now look at the examples of System 2 interventions: (1) derivative inflows paid to System 2 (income-based fees/taxes); and (2) inflation (reduction in purchasing power of currency over time) originating from subsystem 3.

Suppose that one percentage point of income is taken annually in the form of taxes and there is an average of 2% annual inflation over the investment period. This leaves 5% less 3% or **+2%** *net* positive rate of return. The inflation eats at *everyone's* income and savings. In the discussion of subsystem 3 it will be seen how some are at a disadvantage from inflationary policies (**Col E**).

Case #3. Real: Higher Inflation, Taxes Unchanged. Suppose that just as above, about one percentage point of income is taken annually in the form of taxes and there is an average of 5% annual inflation over the investment period. This leaves 5% less 6% or a **-1%** rate of return to be plugged into the formula above.

It might be asked why there are taxes when after deducting for inflation nothing was left over: 5% interest less 5% inflation = *zero real increase in purchasing power*. Taxes are typically computed on *nominal* income and are not adjusted downwards for inflation.

Comparison of Future Values. After the initial investment of 100, the three scenarios are compared for wealth accumulation (W_t) at the end of a specified number of years. Recall that *real* refers to the actual *purchasing power* (more specifically, what can be bought in terms of consumer goods).

End of Year	Case 1 Nominal	Case 2 Real (taxes + inflation)	Case 3 Real (higher inflation)
1	105	102	99
10	165	122	90
20	272	149	82
30	448	182	74

As the table above shows, (Case 2 and 3) higher inflation and taxes tend to reduce the future wealth accumulation because of their impact on rates of return. Recall that inflation is a form of *stealth tax* on holders of the currency subject to dilution.

Deflation. Also recall from the discussion on deflation in the main text, and rates of return in the section on **Wealth Accumulation via Compounding: System 1** that in a deflationary environment (=growth of real purchasing power), in contrast to inflationary environments, *real* purchasing power increases such that the rate of return *increases* (as opposed to *decreasing* with inflation) by the rate of deflation. Thus, in Case #1 above, if annual deflation were 2%, the 2% can be added to the 5% rate of interest being paid by the investment for a *real* rate of return of 7% and greater wealth accumulation. Note however, that the inflation bias of the current monetary system usually means that consistent *overall* purchasing power increases and consumer price deflation are relatively rare, although the cost of certain products have declined.

(6) A Business Entity

Individual Projects. For limited-life projects or assets owned by, a business, C_0 can be an *initial outflow* (cost or outlay) such as a specific *capital investment/expenditure*) with an assumed or targeted *internal rate of return* (IRR) for the project. Depreciation of the asset(s) and scrap value should be considered. If the limited-life asset/project is operated by a business (but is not a business itself to be spun off, for example), forecasting a future value may be less meaningful than evaluating the overall business.

Entire Business. Estimating the future value of an *entire business*, could employ a forecasted IRR of the business based on historical data and trends, etc. Depending on the assumptions, C_0 could be either (1) a contemplated purchase price in an acquisition; or (2) historical annual costs or cash outflows of the business itself (independent of what the business would be purchased for).

An alternative rate of return measure of ongoing business operations is the *rate of return on cost* (RRC) *of the entity itself*. RRC is synchronous, matching annual net cash (in)flows to same-period total cash outflows of the business, (outflows include all *recurring capital expenditures*, business expenses, and acquisitions). See Kennedy (2016: 30, 52-56) for a comparison of the IRR and the RRC. Less than 10 years of historical data may be of limited use.

ADDENDUM

Conventions attempted in the book are mentioned here, although it is recognized that these conventions may not always be consistently applied. **Parentheses.** When a term appears in parentheses after another term [such as *creditors (lenders)*], the meaning of the two terms is taken to be very similar but possibly used in different contexts. The use of "i.e." within parentheses is designed to emphasize the term. "E.g." within parentheses is an abbreviation for "example" as in "for example." Also, "aka" is an abbreviation for "also known as"). Occasionally parentheses will be used in front of or behind another to mean that the word is optional but can help clarify the meaning. **"RE:" or "Re:"** is a *general* reference to an additional source of information related to the topic. Re: is often a concept or terminology, but can also be a work or author that may or may not appear in the *References* section and that should be searchable online. **Slashes.** Like parentheses, a slash (for example, debt/borrowings) means that both terms are nearly identical in meaning in that context and therefore "joined" together by a slash. **Italics** are added because of its deemed importance and often to indicate a technical or other terminology used in the field that could be researched elsewhere for background information. **Boldface** is intended usually to indicate a subtopic. **Currency Units** are at times stated (such as Dollars, Yuan, Euros, Yen) when necessary, but when a neutral example is provided that involves currency, the term "currency units" may also at times be used. **Quotation marks** are used either for emphatic effect, for a popularized term, informal jargon or common expression used in a field, industry, or context. **References** are from a wide variety of sources, academic, practitioner-oriented, and journalistic. It is recognized that using non-academic sources may appear to reduce the quality of the research, but this approach is considered preferable to identify variations in viewpoints--practitioners can offer valuable insights from their first-hand experiences in industry. Quality journalistic references can provide readers with more current information. If a reference is related to a service or organization (e.g. a fund manager, group, political party, etc.), endorsement is not implied. It can be difficult to cover certain topics without referring to research or ideas that might have fallen out of the mainstream, or that are unpopular with certain groups; however, it is hoped that their use can shed light on economic distortions and sustainable, just systems. **Citations**. If the same work is cited in succession, the same work may be indicated only by enclosing the page number in parentheses; it is assumed that the same work is being cited. Some citations are not direct and are sourced from another researcher. It is recognized that a citation may not be representative of, or fully convey, the entirety of a body of research and therefore can be misleading if not qualified. Citing a work doesn't imply approval of, or agreement with, the citation or the cited work or author(s). If the citation is sourced from a fund manager or investment service, although the observation(s) made might be cited, endorsement of that fund or service is not implied. It is not unusual for some historical writings be confusing or inconsistent. It is understood that some educated guesswork may be necessary at times to ascertain what an author most likely intended to say, as even scholars in the field may be unable to fully agree on the meaning of certain passages.

REFERENCES

Abramoviz, M., "Resource and Output Trends in the United States since 1870," *American Economic Review*, Papers and Proceedings, May 1956.

Alesina, Alberto and Giavazzi, Francesco (Eds.), *Fiscal policy after the Financial Crisis*, National Bureau of Economic Research (NBER), University of Chicago Press, 2013.

Altucher James., *The Choose Yourself Guide to Wealth*, CreateSpace Independent Publishing, 2015.

Andrews, Dan., McGowan, Muge Adalet., and Millot, Valentine., "The Walking Dead? Zombie Firms and Productivity Performance in OECD Countries," *OECD Economics Department Working Papers* No. 1372, January 10, 2017.

Aristotle (c. 350 B.C.)., *Politics*, Book III, Chapter 16, Oxford University Press, 2009.

Backhouse, Roger., *A History of Modern Economic Analysis*, Basil Blackwell, Inc., 1987.

Badger, Ralph E., *Valuation of Industrial Securities*, Prentice-Hall, 1925.

Bank for International Settlements (BIS), "Global Financial Markets Remain Dependent on Central Banks," Chapter II, *BIS 85th Annual Report 2014/15*, June 28, 2015, pp. 25-43.

Barro, Robert J., "Are Government Bonds Net Wealth?", *Journal of Political Economy* (Vol. 82, no.6), University of Chicago, Nov/Dec 1974

Bar-Yam, Yaneer., *Making Things Work: Solving Complex Problems in a Complex World*, Knowledge Press, 2005.

Barzun, Jacques., *From Dawn to Decadence: 1500 to the Present: 500 Years of Western Cultural Life*, 1st Ed., Harper Perennial, 2001.

Bastiat, Frédéric (1850)., *The Law*, Tribeca Books, 2015.

Bauer, P.T., *Equality, the Third World and Economic Delusion*, Harvard University Press, Cambridge, Massachusetts, 1981.

Baumol, W.J., Bowen, W.G., "On the Performing Arts: The Anatomy of Their Economic Problems," *The American Economic Review*, Vol. 55, No 1/2. (March 1965), pp. 495-502.

Becker, Gary., *The Economic Approach to Human Behavior*, Chicago: Chicago University Press, 1976.

Bell, Thomas., "The Rule of Law," in Mitchell, Daniel., "The Constitution, Rule of Law and the Power of the Political Class, *International Liberty*, June 5, 2014.

Benson, Bruce L., *The Enterprise of Law: Justice Without the State*, Independent Institute, 2nd Edition, 2011.

Berke, Jeremy., "This Biotech Startup is 3D-Printing Rhino Horns to Try to Stop Poaching," *Business Insider/Science Alert* September 25, 2016.

Berman, Harold J., *Law and Revolution: The Formation of the Western Legal Tradition*, Harvard University Press, 1983.

Bible, Holy see Oxford University Press (Annotated Bible).

Bird, Richard., *Taxing Agricultural Land in Developing Countries*, Harvard University Press, 1974.

BIS, see Bank for International Settlements.

Bohm-Bawerk, E. von., "The Function of Saving" *Annals of the American Academy of Political and Social Science* (May 1901).

Borio, Claudio., Erdem, Magdalena., Filardo, Andrew., Hofmann Boris., "The Cost of Deflations: A Historical Perspective," *BIS Quarterly Review*, March 2015.

Bowles, Samuel., Kirman, Alan., Sethi, Rajiv., "Retrospectives: Friedrich Hayek and the Market Algorithm," *Journal of Economic Perspectives* (Vol. 31 No. 3), Summer, 2017 (pp. 215-30).

Brainard, Lael., "Normalizing Monetary Policy When the Neutral Interest Rate Is Low," *Presentation at the Stanford Institute for Economic Policy Research*, Stanford, California, December 1, 2015.

Brealey, Richard A., and Myers, Stewart., *Principles of Corporate Finance*, The McGraw-Hill Companies, Inc., 1996.

Bregman, Rutger., *Utopia for Realists*, Little, Brown & Company, 2017.

Brown, Gilbert., "Agricultural Pricing Policies and Economic Growth," *Finance and Development*, December 1977.

Brown, Gilbert., "Agricultural Pricing Policies" in Schultz, Theodore (Ed.)., *Distortions of Agricultural Incentives*, 1978.

Cairncross, A.K., *Factors in Economic Development*, London, Allen and Unwin, 1962.

Cantillon, Richard., *Essai sur la Nature du Commerce en Général (traduit de l'anglais)*, 1755.

Chakravarti, Laha, and Roy, (1967). *Handbook of Methods of Applied Statistics,* Volume I, John Wiley and Sons, pp. 392-394. (re: Kolmogorov-Smirnov)

Chandavarkar, Anand G., "Impact of Monetization and Commercialization of the Subsistence Sector on Savings and Credit in Rural Areas," in United Nations, Department of International Economic and Social Affairs, *Savings for Development* (see United Nations).

Chapman, Ben., "Finnish citizens given universal basic income report lower stress levels and greater incentive to work," *The Independent*, June 21, 2017.

Chen, Daphne., "Intermountain, University of Utah Drop EpiPen for Cheaper Alternative," *KSL News*, November 11, 2016.

Chi, Leisha., "Can Toshiba escape fate of corporate Japan's zombie hordes?" *BBC News Business*, April 16, 2017.

Christ, Carl., "A Simple Macroeconomic Model with a Government Budget Restraint," *Journal of Political Economy* 76 (1) (Jan/Feb 1968), 53-67.

Christ, Carl., "On Fiscal and Monetary Policies and the Government Budget Restraint," *The American Economic Review* 69(3-5) (1979), 526-538.

Cirillo, Pasquale., and Taleb, N.N., "On the Statistical Properties and Tail Risk of Violent Conflicts," Tail Risk Working Papers, *ArXiv*, Oct 19, 2015.

Cirillo, Pasquale., Fontanari, Andrea., and Taleb, Nassim, Nicholas., "Gini estimation under infinite variance," Tail Risk Research Program, *ArXiv*, July 9, 2017.

Clarida, Richard., "Removing Accommodation" *PIMCO Global Central Bank Focus*, March 2017.

Cobb, C. W.; Douglas, P. H. (1928). "A Theory of Production". *American Economic Review* 18 (Supplement): 139–165.

Cohen, Jerome B. and Zinbarg, Edward D.., *Investment Analysis and Portfolio Management*, Richard D. Irwin, Inc., Homewood, Illinois 1967.

Coltman, Michael M., *Buying & Selling a Small Business*, International Self Counsel Press, Ltd., 3rd Ed., 1991.

Cook, John. D., "Thick Tails," *John D. Cook Applied Mathematics Consulting* (johndcook.com), January 18, 2008.

Cook, John D., "Quantile-Quantile Plots and Powers of 3/2," *John D. Cook Applied Mathematics Consulting* (johndcook.com), April 2, 2017.

Coyne, Christopher and Coyne, Rachel (Eds.)., *Flaws and Ceilings: Price Controls and the Damage They Cause*, Institute of Economic Affairs, 2015.

Cramer, James J., *Real Money*, Simon & Schuster, 2009.

Creveld, Martin (van), *The Rise and Decline of the State*, Cambridge University Press, 1999.

Crook, Clive., "World Economy Survey," *The Economist*, September 20, 1997.

Damodaran, Aswath., *Investment Valuation.*, John Wiley & Sons, Inc., 1996, (3rd Ed.) 2012.

Davis, Nicola., "Why Roman concrete still stands strong while modern version decays," *The Guardian*, July 4, 2017.

De Bonilla, Gabriela Vargas., "La Agricultura" in *La Costa de Chiapas: Un Estudio Económico Regional*, Universidad Nacional Autonóma de México, 1974.

De La Calle, L.S., (1544) *Instrucción de Mercaderes* ... (see Grice-Hutchinson 1952)

Denison, E.F., *Accounting for US Economic Growth 1929-69*, Washington, Brookings Institution, 1974.

Devajaran, Shantayanan, and Anthony C. Fisher., "Hotelling's Economics of Exhaustible Resources: Fifty Years Later," *Journal of Economic Literature* Vol. XIX (March 1981), 65-73.

Dewing, Arthur Stone., *The Financial Policy of Corporations*, 5th Ed., The Ronald Press, 1953.

Diamandis, Peter, and Kotler, Steven., *Abundance: The Future is Better Than You Think*, Free Press, 2014.

Dixon, Peter B. and Jorgenson, Dale., *Handbook of Computable General Equilibrium Modeling*, Volume 1A, Elsevier North Holland, 2013.

Dorsey, Pat., *The Five Rules for Successful Stock Investing: Morningstar's Guide to Building Wealth and Winning in the Market*, Morningstar, Inc., 1994.

Douady, R., and N.N. Taleb., "A Map and Simple Heuristic to Detect Fragility, Antifragility, and Model Error," *arXiv Preprint*, 2012.

Economist (of London), "Sahel, Bitter Harvest?", January 29, 1983: 76-7.

Eicher, Carl K., "Africa's Food Crisis," *Foreign Affairs*, Fall 1982.

Eisenhardt, Kathleen M., "Agency Theory: An Assessment and Review," *Academy of Management Review* (Vol 14, No. 1), 1989, pp. 57-74.

El-Erian, Mohamed., *The Only Game in Town: Central Banks, Instability and Avoiding the Next Collapse*, Random House, New York, 2016.

Faber, Marc., *Tomorrow's Gold: Asia's Age of Discovery*, CLSA Books, 2010.

Fabozzi, Frank J., The Handbook of *Fixed Income Securities, 8th Edition,* McGraw-Hill, 2011.

Fabozzi, Frank J., and Modigliani, Franco., *Capital Markets: Institutions and Instruments,* Prentice-Hall, Inc., 1992.

Fama, E., and Jensen, M., "Separation of Ownership and Control," *Journal of Law and Economics* (26: 301-325), 1983.

Fellman, Philip Vos., Bar-Yam, Yaneer, Minai, Ali A., Editors., *Conflict and Complexity*, Springer, 2016.

Ferguson, Niall., "How Great Powers Fall," Newsweek, December 7, 2009 (41-44).

Ferguson, Niall., *The Great Degeneration*, Penguin Books, 2014.

Ferriss, Timothy., *Tools of Titans: The Tactics, Routines, and Habits of Billionaires, Icons and World-Class Performers,* Houghton Mifflin Harcourt, 2016.

Fetter, Frank A., "Interest Theories, Old and New," *The American Economic Review*, Volume IV, No. 1 (March 1914), 68-92.

Financial Times, "Definition of Principal/Agent Problem," *Financial Times Lexicon* (undated), 2017.

Fisher, I., *The Theory of Interest (as Determined by Impatience to Spend Income and Opportunity to Invest It)*, New York: The Macmillan Company, 1930.

Forrester, Jay., "Counterintuitive Behavior of Social Systems," *Technology Review* 73 (3) 52-68, 1971.

Friedman, David D., Future Imperfect, Cambridge University Press, 1st Ed., 2008.

Friedman, David D., Law's Order: What Economics Has to Do with Law and Why It Matters, Princeton University Press, 2001.

Friedman, Milton., *Price Theory*, Walter de Gruyter: Aldine Publishing Company, 1986.

GAO (see General Accounting Office).

Gates, Bill., *Bill Gates: The Life, Lessons & Rules for Success*, Independent Publisher, 2017. (also see Small, Cathleen, Re: Melinda Gates)

General Accounting Office (GAO), *U.S., Report to Congress: Disincentives to Agricultural Production in Developing Countries*, November 26, 1975.

Goldberg, Jonah., *Liberal Fascism*, Crown Forum, 2009.

Gordon, M., *The Investment, Financing and Valuation of the Corporation*, Richard D. Irwin, Inc., Homewood, Illinois, 1962. (Re: Gordon Growth Model)

Graham, Benjamin., (1949) *The Intelligent Investor: The Classic Text on Value Investing*, Harper Business, 2005.

Grant, James., *Mr. Market Miscalculates: The Bubble Years and Beyond*, Axios Press, 2008.

Grant, James., *The Trouble with Prosperity*, Times Books/Random House, 1996.

Greenblatt, Joel., *The Little Book that Beats the Market*, John Wiley & Sons, 2006.

Grice-Hutchinson, M. (1952)., The *School of Salamanca: Readings in Spanish Monetary Theory, 1544-1605*, 1952. (also see Hutchison, Terence)

Gupta, Girish., "Venezuela money supply surges 10 percent in one week, fastest in 25 years," *Reuters*, July 29, 2017.

Hale, Thomas., "Pension Funds Turn to Mortgage Market in Search of Higher Yield, *Financial Times*, December 17, 2015.

Hahm, Melody., "This Golf Course is Being Converted into a Residential Olive Grove," *Yahoo Finance*, August 22, 2017.

Hanke, Steve H., "Venezuela: No Rule of Law, Bad Money," *Globe Asia*, May-June 2015 (reprinted: Cato Institute, Commentary).

Hanke, Steve H., "Venezuela's Grim Reaper -- A Weekly Report," *Zero Hedge*, August 29, 2017.

Harcourt, G.C and Laing, N.F., (Eds.) *Capital and Growth*, Harmondsworth: Penguin, 1971.

Hayek, Friedrich A., *Prices and Production,* London: Routledge, Kegan & Paul, 1931.

Hayek, Friedrich A., (1944) *The Road to Serfdom*, University of Chicago Press, 2007.

Hayek, Friedrich A., (1974), "The Pretense of Knowledge," essay presented at the occasion of Hayek's Nobel Prize in Economics, December 11, 1974, reprinted with permission by the Foundation for Economic Education (FEE).

Hayek, Friedrich A., "The Use of Knowledge in Society," *The American Economic Review*, Vol. 35, No. 4 (September 1945), pp. 519-530.

Heimann, Eduard., *History of Economic Doctrines*, Oxford University Press, 1964.

Herrick, Devon M., "Regulations and Bureaucracy Boosted EpiPen Prices," *Statement, Reviewing the Rising Price of EpiPens*, House Committee on Oversight & Government Reform, September 21, 2016.

Hessen, Dag O., and Wilson, David., "Blueprint for the Global Village," *Journal of Cliodynamics*, 5 (1):123-157, 2014.

Hicks, J.R., *Value and Capital*, 2nd Ed., Clarendon Press, Oxford, 1946.

Hitchner, James R., *Financial Valuation: Applications and Models*, 3rd Ed., John Wiley & Sons, 2011.

Hoffer, Eric (1951)., *The True Believer: Thoughts on the Nature of Mass Movements*, Harper Perennial Modern Classics, 2010

Hollingsworth, Barbara. "Economist Tells Congress: U.S. May Be in 'Worse Fiscal Shape' Than Greece," *CNS News*, March 9, 2015. (See Kotlikoff, 2015)

Hoppe, Hans-Hermann., *The Economics and Ethics of Private Property*, Ludwig von Mises Institute, 1993, 2006.

Hopper, W. David., essay in Schulz, Theodore W. (Ed.) *Distortions of Agricultural Incentives* (1978).

Hotelling, Harold., "The Economics of Exhaustible Resources," *The Journal of Political Economy* 39 (2) (April 1931), 137-175.

Huerta de Soto, Jesus., *Money, Bank Credit, and Economic Cycles*, Ludwig von Mises Institute, 2012.

Human Rights Council, Written statement submitted by the Global Alliance Against Traffic in Women, a non-governmental organization in special consultative status, Twenty-Third Session, Agenda item 3, United Nations General Assembly, May 17, 2013. (also see Reisenwitz, Cathy)

Hussman, John P., "Estimating Market Losses at a Speculative Extreme," *Hussman Funds Weekly Market Comment*, August 7, 2017.

Hutchison, Terence., *Before Adam Smith: The Emergence of Political Economy*, 1662-1776, Basil Blackwell, Ltd., 1988.

Hutt, William., *A Rehabilitation of Say's Law*, Ohio University Press: Athens, 1974. (Also see Manhattan Institute, 1983)

International Monetary Fund, "*IMF World Economic Outlook (WEO)*, April 2015.

International Monetary Fund, "United States: Selected Issues Paper," *IMF Country Report* No. 10/248, July 2010.

Johnson N.I., "Systems of Frequency Curves Generated by Methods of Translation," *Biometrika* (36:149-176), 1949.

Johnson, Sarah., and Leone, Marie., "Congress Members Fume at Fair Value," *CFO Newsletters*, March 12, 2009.

Kamuanga, Malumba., "Farm level Study of the Rice Production Systems at the Office de Niger in Mali: An Economic Analysis," Michigan, 1982 (cited in Eicher, Carl "Africa's Food Crisis" 1982)

Kennedy, Raoul., *Equity Income Analytics*, Amazon Publishing, LLC, 2014.

Kennedy, Raoul., *Interest Rate Analytics*, Amazon Publishing, LLC, 2015.

Kennedy, Raoul., *Rate-of-Return Analytics*, Amazon Publishing, LLC, 2016.

Keynes, John Maynard., *The General Theory of Employment, Interest, and Money,* London: Macmillan, 1936.

Klein, Lawrence R., *The Economics of Supply and Demand*, Basil Blackwell Publisher Limited, 1983.

Knight, Frank., (1921) *Risk, Uncertainty and Profit*, LSE reprints of scarce tracts, London, LSE [as cited in Backhouse (1987) and Friedman (1986)].

Kotlikoff, Lawrence J., "America's Fiscal Insolvency and Its Generational Consequences," *Testimony to the Senate Budget Committee*, 2015.

Kurzweil, Ray., "The Law of Accelerating Returns," (kurzweilai.net/the-law-of-accelerating-returns), March 7, 2001.

Kuznets, Simon., *Modern Economic Growth: Rate Structure and Spread*, New Haven, Yale University Press, 1966.

Laubach, Thomas, Williams., John C., "Measuring the Natural Rate of Interest Redux" *Federal Reserve Bank of San Francisco Working Paper Series 2015-16*, October 2015.

Laubach, Thomas, Williams, John C., "Measuring the Natural Rate of Interest," *Review of Economics and Statistics* (Vol 85, No. 4: 1063-1070) November 2003.

Leamer, E.E., "Let's Take the Con out of Econometrics," *American Economic Review*, 73 (1983), 31-43.

Leoni, Bruno (1961)., *Freedom and the Law*, (3rd Ed., expanded) Liberty Fund, 1991; 1st Ed., Princeton: d. Van Nostrand, 1961.
(Also see Rothbard, Murray., *"On Freedom and the Law"*)

Lévy, Bernard-Henri., *La Barbarie à Visage Humain*, B. Grasset, 1977 (English and French version Livre de Poche, 1985)

Lichtenfeld, Marc., *Get Rich with Dividends*, John Wiley & Sons, Inc., 2nd.Edition, 2015.

Lindahl, Erik., *Studies in the Theory of Money and Capital* (Translation: Tor Ferholm), London: Allen & Unwin, 1939.

Locke, John (1668) as cited in Hutchison (1988: 63). See Hutchison, Terence.

Locke, John (1689)., *Second Treatise on Government* (Chap. IV: 22), Hackett, 1980.

Lofchie, Michael F., (1978a) "Political and Economic Origins of African Hunger," *The Journal of Modern African Studies.*, 13:4 1978.

Lofchie, Michael F., (1978b) "Agrarian Crisis and Economic Liberalization in Tanzania," *The Journal of Modern African Studies*, 163 1978.

Lucas, Robert (1976). "Econometric Policy Evaluation: A Critique". In Brunner, K.; Meltzer, A. *The Phillips Curve and Labor Markets*. Carnegie-Rochester Conference Series on Public Policy 1. New York: American Elsevier. pp. 19–46.

Lundvall, Henrik., and Westermark, Andreas, "What is the Natural Interest Rate?" *Sveriges Riksbank Economic Review* (2011:2).

Madison, James (1788)., Federalist No.62, *The Federalist Papers*, Dover Publications, 2014.

Malkiel, Burton., *A Random Walk Down Wall Street: The Time-Tested Strategy for Successful Investing*, (11th Edition), W.W. Norton & Company, 2016.

Malthus, Thomas. (1815), *An Inquiry into the Nature and Progress of Rent*, as cited in Winch (1987) Oxford University Press.

Manhattan Institute for Policy Research, "Hutt: An Economist for This Century", *Manhattan Report on Economic Policy*, Vol III No. 5., 1983.

Manhattan Institute for Policy Research, "On the Brink: Third World Economies in Crisis," *Manhattan Report*, January 1983.

Manrique, Marta., Marqués, José Manuel., "An Empirical Approximation of the Natural Rate of Interest and Potential Growth" *Documento de Trabajo No. 0416*, Banco de España, Madrid, 2004.

Markowitz, H.M., "Portfolio Selection," *The Journal of Finance* 7 (1): 77–91, March 1952.

Marx, Karl (1867)., *Capital: Volume 1: A Critique of Political Economy*, Penguin Classics; Reprint Edition (1992).

McCloskey, Dierdre N., "The Core of Liberty is Economic Liberty," *Foundation for Economic Education*, September 7, 2017.

McCormick, Liz., "Global Bond Rally Near 'Panic' Level with Japan Yield Below Zero," *Bloomberg Business*, Feb 9, 2016.

McKinnon, Ronald I., *Money & Capital in Economic Development,* Brooking Institution Press, 1973.

McKinsey Global Institute, "Debt and (Not Much) Deleveraging," *MGI Report*, McKinsey & Company, February 2015.

Miller, Merton H., and Charles W. Upton., "A Test of the Hotelling Valuation Principle," *Journal of Political Economy* 93 (1), 1985.

Mill, John Stuart (1848)., *Principles of Political Economy*, Books IV and V, Penguin Group, 1988. (Original 1848)

Mill, John Stuart (1859)., *On Liberty*, Dover Publications, 2002.

Mises, Ludwig von., (1912) *The Theory of Money and Credit* (translated from the German) 1934; also, Yale University Press, 1953.

Mises, Ludwig von., (1920) Economic *Calculation in the Socialist Commonwealth* (original: "*Die Wirtschaftrechnung im sozialistischen Gemeinwesen*", *Archiv fur Sozialwissenschaften* 47 (1920)), Ludwig von Mises Institute, 2012.

Mises, Ludwig von., (1944) *Bureaucracy*, Yale University Press, 1944; Liberty Fund, 2007.

Mitchell, "The Constitution, Rule of Law and the Power of the Political Class, *International Liberty*, June 5, 2014

Mitchell, Daniel., (2017a) "Social Security's Creeping Fiscal Crisis," *International Liberty*, July 17, 2017.

Mitchell, Daniel., (2017b) "To Fight Cronyism, Let's Have Separation of Business and State," *International Liberty*, August 24, 2017.

Moody's Investors Service Global Credit Research, "Putting EBITDA in Perspective," *Special Comment*, June 2000.

Murray, Charles., *Coming Apart: The State of White America, 1960-2010*, Crown Forum, 2013.

Myint, H., *The Economics of the Developing Countries*, Hutchinson University Library, 1980.

Myrdal, Gunnar, *Monetary Equilibrium* (Translation: R.B. Bryce and N. Stolper), London: William Hodge & Company, 1939.

National Institute of Standards and Technology (NIST), Exploratory Data Analysis, EDA Techniques, Quantitative Techniques (1.3.5.14, 1.3.5.15, 1.3.5.16), *NIST/SEMATECH e-Handbook of Statistical Methods*, 2012. (*See references to goodness of fit testing)

Neumann, J.V., "A Model of General Economic Equilibrium," *The Review of Economic Studies*, Vol. 13 No.1 (1945-46), pp 1-9.

Niño, José, "Venezuela Before Chavez: A Prelude to Socialist Failure," *Mises Wire*, May 4, 2017

Niño, José, Venezuela: Forty Years of Economic Decline," *Mises Wire*, May 17, 2017

NIST, see National Institute of Standards and Technology.

Nordhaus, William D., "Baumol's Diseases: A Macroeconomic Perspective," *NBER Working Paper* No. 12218, Issued in May 2006

North, Gary., *Marx's Religion of Revolution: Regeneration Through Chaos*, Institute for Christian Economics, 1989.

OECD, *National Income Accounts at a Glance*, Organisation for Economic Cooperation and Development, 2014.

Olson, Mancur., *The Logic of Collective Action: Public Goods and the Theory of Groups*, Harvard University Press, Revised Edition, 1971.

Organisation for Economic Cooperation and Development (see OECD).

Orwell, George (1951)., *1984*, Signet Classic, 1961.

Ottaway, Marina., "Soviet Marxism and African Socialism," *Journal of Modern African Studies*, 16, 3 1978.

Oxford University Press., *The New Oxford Annotated Bible New Revised Standard Version with the Apocrypha*, Oxford University Press, 2001.

Paddock, William, and Paul., *Famine 1975!* Little, Brown & Co., 1967.

Panico, Carlo., *Interest and Profit in the Theories of Value and Distribution*, The Macmillan Press, Ltd., 1988.

Parkinson, Joe., "Kenya Election ruling May be Watershed for African Democracy," *The Wall Street Journal*, September 4, 2017.

Perkins, John., *Confessions of an Economic Hit Man*, Plume, 2005.

Perkins, John., *New Confessions of an Economic Hit Man*, Berrett-Koehler Publishers, 2016.

Perry, Mark., "Don't Outlaw Price Gouging After Harvey. Let the Market Work," Opinion, *Newsweek*, August 28, 2017.

Petersen, William., "The Social Roots of Hunger and Overpopulation," *The Public Interest*, No. 68, Summer 1982.

Peters, Josh., "Dividends, Cash and TINA," *Morningstar DividendInvestor,* Morningstar, Inc. (Vol. 12, No. 6), July 2016.

Peters, Josh., *The Ultimate Dividend Playbook*, Morningstar, Inc., 2008.

Piketty, Thomas., *Capitalism in the Twenty-First Century*, Harvard University Press, Cambridge, Mass., 2014.

Pindyck, Robert S., and Rubinfeld, Daniel L., *Econometric Models and Economic Forecasts*, McGraw-Hill International, 1991.

Pinker, Steven., *The Better Angels of Our Nature: Why Violence Has Declined*, Penguin Books, 2012.

Pratt, Shannon P., *Valuing a Business*, 2nd Ed., Business One Irwin, 1989.

Raico, Ralph (Ed.)., *New Individualist Review (1961)*, Indianapolis: Liberty Fund, 1981.

Rake, Alan., "The Collapse of African Agriculture," *African Development*, February 1975.

Rand, Ayn., *Capitalism: The Unknown Ideal*, The New American Library, 1966.

Rauch, Johnathan., *Demosclerosis*, Crown Publishing, 1994.

Reisenwitz, Cathy., "Walking the Red-Light District", Foundation for Economic Education (FEE), July 27, 2014.

Reisman, George., *Why Nazism was Socialism and Why Socialism is Totalitarian*, TJS Books, 2014.

Reisman, George., *Capitalism: A Treatise on Economics*, TJS Books, 1996.

Ricardo, David (1826)., (P. Sraffa, Ed. with M. Dobb)., *The Works and Correspondence of David Ricardo, Volume I: On the Principles of Political Economy and Taxation*, Cambridge: Cambridge University Press, 1951-1983.

Rickards, James., *Currency Wars: The Making of the Next Global Crisis*, Portfolio, 2012

Rickards, James., *The Death of Money: The Coming Collapse of the International Monetary System*, Portfolio, 2017.

Rifkin, Jeremy., *The End of Work: The Decline of the Global Labor Force and the Dawn of the Post-Market Era*, Tarcher, 1996.

Romer, David., "Dynamic Stochastic General Equilibrium Models of Fluctuations". *Advanced Macroeconomics* (Fourth ed.). New York: McGraw-Hill Irwin, pp. 312–364, 2012.

Ropke, Wilhelm., *Crises and Cycles* (adapted and revised by Vera C. Smith), William Hodge and Co. Ltd., 1936.

Rosenbaum, Joshua., Pearl, Joshua., *Investment Banking: Valuation, Leveraged Buyouts and Mergers & Acquisitions*, (2nd Ed.), 2013.

Ross, Stephen A., "The Arbitrage Theory of Capital Asset Pricing". *Journal of Economic Theory* 13 (3):341–360, 1976.

Ross, Stephen A., Westerfield, Randolph W., Jaffe, Jeffrey., *Corporate Finance*, 8th Ed., McGraw-Hill Irwin, 2008.

Rothbard, Murray., "Breaking out of the Walrasian Box: The Cases of Schumpeter and Hansen," *The Review of Austrian Economics*, Spring 1987, pp 97-108.

Rothbard, Murray., "Time Preference" in *Capital Theory* (John Eatwell, Murray Milgate, and Peter Newman, Eds.), W.W. Norton & Company, 1990.

Rothbard, Murray., "On Freedom and the Law," in Raico, Ralph (Ed.), *New Individualist Review (1961)*, Indianapolis: Liberty Fund, 1981.

Rummel, R.J., *Death by Government: Genocide and Mass Murder Since 1900*, Routledge, 1997.

Russo, Camila., "Ethereum Co-Founder Says Crypto Coin Market Is a Time Bomb," *Bloomberg Technology*, July 18, 2017.

Salerno, Joseph T., "The Fed and Bernanke Are Wrong About the Natural Interest Rate," *Mises Wire*, June 26, 2016.

Say, J.B., *Traité d'Economie Politique*, 1803.

Sayama, Hiroki., *Introduction to the Modeling and Analysis of Complex Systems*, Open SUNY Textbooks, Milne Library, 2015.

Schilt, James H., "A Rational Approach to Capitalization Rates for Discounting the Future Income Stream of Closely Held Companies, " *The Financial Planner*, Jan. 1982.

Schultz, Theodore W., (Ed) *Distortions of Agricultural Incentives*, Indiana University Press, 1978.

Scott, Maurice FitzGerald., *A New View of Economic Growth*, Oxford University Press, 1989.

Serra, Antonio (1613*).*, *A Brief Treatise on the Causes which can make Gold and Silver Plentiful in Kingdoms where there are No Mines*, cited in Hutchison (1988) from Monroe A.E. (1924) *Early Economic Thought*.

Sethi, Ramit., *I Will Teach you to be Rich*, Workman Publishing Company, 2009.

Shedlock, Michael., "Zombie Corporations Litter Europe, Kept Alive by ECB," *Zero Hedge*, July 30, 2017 (originally published in MishTalk, July 29, 2017).

Shim, Jae K., Siegel, Joel G., and Simon, Abraham J., et al., *The Vest-Pocket MBA*, Prentice-Hall, Inc., 1986.

Shuh, Edward., "Equity-Motivated Policies as Distortions," in Schulz, Theodore W., *Distortions of Agricultural Incentives*, 1978.

Shultz, Theodore W., *Distortions of Agricultural Incentives*, Bloomington, Indiana University Press, 1978.

Schumpeter, J.A. (1954)., *History of Economic Analysis,* Oxford University Press, 1996.

Sigurjónsson, Frosti., *Monetary Reform: A Better Monetary System for Iceland,* Reykjavik, Iceland, March 2015. (Report commissioned by the Prime Minister of Iceland, Edition 1.0, 2015).

Small, Cathleen., *Melinda Gates: Philanthropist and Education Advocate (Leading Women)*, Cavendish Square Publishing, 2017.

Smirnov, Sergey., "Economic Fluctuations in Russia (from the late 1920s to 2015)," *Russian Journal of Economics*, (Volume 1, Issue 2, 130-153) June 2015 (article posted in *ScienceDirect*).

Smith, Adam (1776), *An Inquiry into the Nature and Causes of the Wealth of Nations*, David Campbell Publishers Ltd., 1991 and University of Chicago Press, 1976.

Smith, Charles Hugh., *A Radically Beneficial World: Automation, Technology, and Creating Jobs for All: The Future Belongs to Work That is Meaningful*, CreateSpace Independent Publishing, 2015.

Snedecor, George W. and Cochran, William G., *Statistical Methods*, Eighth Edition, Iowa State University Press, 1989. (re: Chi-Square)

Solís, Leopoldo., *Economic policy Reform in Mexico: A Case Study for Developing Countries*, Pergamon Press, 1981.

Solow, Robert., "Building a Science of Economics for the Real World," *Prepared Statement of Robert Solow, Professor Emeritus,*

MIT, to the House Committee on Science and Technology, Subcommittee on Investigations and Oversight, July 20, 2010.

Solow, Robert., "Capital Theory and the Rate of Return," in Harcourt, G.C and Laing, N.F., (Eds.) *Capital and Growth.* Harmondsworth: Penguin, 1971.

Solow, Robert M., "Technical Change and the Aggregate Production Function," *Review of Economics and Statistics*, August 1957.

Sowell, Thomas., *Say's Law*, Oxford University Press, 1973.

Sowell, Thomas., *The Vision of the Anointed: Self-Congratulation as a Basis for Social Policy*, Basic Books, 1996.

Sowell, Thomas., *The Quest for Cosmic Justice*, Free Press, 2002.

Sowell, Thomas., *A Conflict of Visions: Ideological Origins of Political Struggles*, Basic Books, 2007.

Spiegel, Murray R., Schiller, John., and Srinivasan, R. Alu., *Probability and Statistics*, 2nd Edition, Tata McGraw-Hill, 2006.

Spitznagel, Mark., "What Is This "Neutral" Interest Rate Touted by the Fed?", *Mises Wire*, January 3, 2017.

Spitznagel, Mark., "Why Cryptocurrencies Will Never Be Safe Havens," *Mises Wire*, August 14, 2017.

Stephens, M. A. (1974). "EDF Statistics for Goodness of Fit and Some Comparisons," *Journal of the American Statistical Association*, 69, pp. 730-737. (re: Anderson-Darling)

Stevens, Charles J., "Confronting the World Food Crisis," *Occasional Paper 27*, Stanley Foundation, December 1981.

Stigler, George J., *The Theory of Price*, 4th Ed., Macmillan Publishing Co., 1987.

Stockman, David., "Soon Comes the Deluge," *Contra Corner*, January 19, 2016.

Stockman, David., *The Great Deformation: The Corruption of Capitalism in America*, PublicAffairs™, 2013.

Takeo, Yuko., Jeong Lee Ming., Hasegawa, Toshiro., "Japan's Central Bank is Distorting the Market, Bourse Chief Says," *Bloomberg*, July 20, 2017.

Taleb, Nassim Nicholas., *The Black Swan*, Random House Trade Paperbacks, 2010.

Taleb, Nassim Nicholas., *Antifragile: Things That Gain from Disorder*, Random House, 2012.

Taleb, Nassim Nicholas., (2016a) "The Most Intolerant Wins: The Dictatorship of the Small Minority," *Medium*, August 14, 2016.

Taleb, Nassim Nicholas., (2016b) "Inequality and Skin in the Game," *Medium*, December 28, 2016.

Theil, Peter., *Zero to One: Notes on Startups, or How to Build the Future*, Crown Business, 2014.

Trautwein, Hans-Michael., "Interest, Neutral Rate of," *International Encyclopedia of the Social Sciences*, Thomson Gale, 2008.

Tuller, Lawrence W., *The Small Business Valuation Book*, Adams Media, 1994.

United Nations, Department of International Economic and Social Affairs, *Savings for Development*, Report of the International Symposium on the Mobilization of Personal Savings in Developing Countries (Feb 1980), © New York, 1981.

United States Department of Agriculture (USDA), "Foods Typically Purchased by Supplemental Nutrition Assistance Program (SNAP) Households, *Nutrition Assistance Program Report*, Office of Policy Support, Food and Nutrition Service (submitted by IMPAQ International, LLC), November 2016.

USDA, see United States Department of Agriculture.

Van Creveld, Martin (see Creveld)

Von Mises, von Hayek., see Mises, Hayek.

Voslensky, Michael., *Nomenklatura: The Soviet Ruling Class*, Doubleday, 1984.

Walker, Francis A., *Political Economy*, Henry Holt and Company, New York, 1888.

White, Lawrence., "Antifragile Banking and Monetary Systems," *Cato Journal*, Vol. 33, No. 3 (Fall 2013), 471-484.

Wickens, Michael., *Macroeconomic Theory: A Dynamic General Equilibrium Approach*, Second Edition, Princeton University Press, 2011.

Wicksell, Knut., *Geldzins und Guterpreise*, (Interest and Prices) Jena, 1898 (English-language translations 1936, 1965: Interest and Prices, New York, Kelley 1965).

Winch, Donald., *Malthus*, Oxford University Press, 1987.

World Bank, "Accelerated Development in Sub-Saharan Africa," Washington, 1981: 55.

Young, Crawford., *Ideology and Development in Africa*, Yale University Press, 1982.

Additional Notes, Resources, and Acknowledgements

Some references contained herein were used also in Kennedy (2016) or are intended for use in upcoming work. Interest rate data were sourced from the Board of Governors of the Federal Reserve System (US) online databases. Annual financial statements of firms are sourced from the filings with the U.S. Securities and Exchange Commission (SEC) or from company annual reports containing financial statements. The NASDAQ, Wikipedia, Wikinvest, Econ Library (econlib.org), Investing dot com, and Yahoo Finance websites were consulted for financial and other information. Special thanks to systemdynamics.org, article contributions within *social complexity* group discussions and the Taipei Institute of Banking and Finance.

www.ingramcontent.com/pod-product-compliance
Lightning Source LLC
Chambersburg PA
CBHW050207230526
45470CB00001B/272